Revealing the
Non-Secrets

To Brother Jim Simpkins —

With sincere appreciation for his
genuine brotherhood and dedication

to Delta Upsilon —

Fraternally,

Houston '92

Revealing the Non-Secrets

The History of the Founding and
Founders of Delta Upsilon Fraternity

Craig S. Sowell

Foreword By
General Tommy R. Franks (Ret.)

Published in 2009 by Createspace

FIRST EDITION

_____

Sowell, Craig S.
    Revealing the Non-Secrets: The History of the Founding and Founders of Delta Upsilon Fraternity / Craig S. Sowell. – 1st ed.

    ISBN   1440473544
    EAN-13   9781440473548

    1. History – Fraternity

For more information on this book, or to purchase additional copies, visit the book's website at: https://www.createspace.com/3360786

To Robin, Laura and Matthew...

...to anyone who proudly wears
the Badge of Delta Upsilon ...

...and to our Founders,
may they never be forgotten...

Contents

"I can think of no one in the realm of Delta Upsilon International Fraternity more perfect to tell the wonderful account of our Fraternity's Founding History than Brother Craig Sowell. From his enthusiastic days as an undergraduate, I have watched him live-out his love for DU as an alumnus and fraternity professional.

This exceptional educational tool on the beginnings of our beloved fraternity will educate DUs and the entire fraternity world as we seek to establish our relevance in the 21st Century. Every Chapter of Delta Upsilon and every chapter of our interfraternal brother's and sister's fraternities and sororities would be wise to have its members read this compelling story of men who believed that what they had created was too good to hide, too life changing to keep secret, and wildly immortal past their precious lives as Founders.

Let us all read this book and be moved to do something great in our lives!"

Will Keim, PhD.
Pacific '75

Acknowledgements

Most books have this section in the back of the book. I have chosen to put it in the front, however, so that these fine folks listed below will not be as easily overlooked. Without their assistance, many facts in this book would have neither been discovered nor confirmed. Each of these individuals was most gracious with their time and patience. Their support for this book is acknowledged with sincere appreciation.

Very heartfelt thanks to the wonderful **Linda Hall**, Archives Assistant at the Williams College Library. Her extremely adept skill for research, her pleasant communication and sincere help are a large reason why our DU Founders have an identity in this book. This book would be nothing more than a pamphlet without her help. I offer her an enormous amount of thanks on behalf of a grateful Fraternity.

The following people also deserve a sincere thank you for their involvement in the development of this book:

Rev. Peter Bridgford, *Northwestern '56*
Aaron D. Clevenger, *Central Florida '97*
Jana Cole
Adam L. Culley, *Northern Iowa '00*
Jeffrey L. Fuhrman, *Northern Iowa '94*
Brian K. Erickson, *Houston '96*
Barbara A. Harness
Joshua A. Katz, *Central Florida '97*
Robert S. Lannin, *Nebraska '81*
Dave Maguire, *Southern Illinois '73*
Stephen K. Rowley, *Ohio '65*
David R. Schumacher
Melinda B. Sopher
Richard X. Taylor, *North Carolina State '82*

The following citizens either led me to a piece of valuable information or went above and beyond the call of duty to provide a critical element:

Bob Avery – Great Barrington, Massachusetts
Steven P. Blackburn – Hartford, Connecticut
Jane Cady – Hampton, Illinois
Cynthia Cosgrove – Easthampton, Massachusetts
Felecie O. Joyce – Sheffield, Massachusetts
Joan Kauffman – Cambridge, Massachusetts
Barbara LaBombard – Easthampton, Massachusetts
David Allen Lambert – Boston, Massachusetts
Rusty Lanzit – Chaplin, Connecticut
Eileen Lowney – Fairhaven, Massachusetts
Linda Marshall – Ogdensburg, New York
Nancy Melville – Glendale, Ohio
June Persing – Plainfield, Massachusetts
Sally Powers-Albertz – Fond du Lac, Wisconsin
Ella S. Pozell – Washington, D.C.
Lori Reynolds – Easthampton, Massachusetts
Orin Rockhold – Moline, Illinois
Melanie Rosenbaum – Sharon, Massachusetts
Marie A. Rovero – Hartford, Connecticut
Linda Thorpe – Monterey, Massachusetts
Hollis Warner – Riverhead, New York

Special thanks to Brothers Lou Holtz, Tommy Franks and Will Keim for their support for this book, which is made better by their association.

...And finally, to Chris Einspahr, *Houston '94*, who first invited me to the Delta Upsilon chapter house on a warm summer evening in Houston, Texas. I have been a better man ever since, thanks to DU and your invitation.

Foreword

"The challenge of history is to recover the past and introduce it to the present." That quote by Professor David Thelen probably sums up best, the efforts of this book's author. Brother Craig Sowell has, in effect, single-handedly recovered the past of Delta Upsilon's Founding and put it into a format to introduce it to the present generation.

Brother Sowell paints a wonderful picture of the Fraternity's Founding in this book, and has done a masterful job of ensuring that the legacy of the Founders will be preserved for future generations. Our Delta Upsilon Founders are forgotten no longer, and their efforts are now fully recorded for posterity.

When I joined Delta Upsilon at the University of Texas, I cannot recall ever really learning about the Founders of our Fraternity, or the story of the Founding itself. Now I know why. The story had never been written down...until now. The Founders themselves were faceless to us...until now. The story of <u>how</u> they began, of <u>why</u> they began, and of <u>what</u> they began, has been rescued. The pieces of the puzzle have been put back together to paint a wonderful history of the early days of our great Fraternity, and of the men who took a stance on that first day.

I have always believed that leaders are not born, but that they are developed. I believe that to be even truer of our Founders. The education and discipline that they received, the character that they possessed and the moral compass within them, helped to guide them in their quest for something better, something different. Their grit and determination helped pave the way for those of us who would follow them, so that we who were not born leaders, could be developed into leaders. Delta Upsilon did then, as it does today...build leaders for tomorrow.

Now our early story can at last be told. I am proud to know that future generations of DU Brothers will be able to benefit from this fantastic information.

<u>Revealing the Non-Secrets</u> is, without a doubt, a Delta Upsilon Fraternity treasure.

General Tommy R. Franks, *Texas '67*
United States Army (Ret.)

Preface

Since our beginning in 1834, the Delta Upsilon Fraternity has produced a history of the organization every fifty years. Mathematically up to this point, that would make three books on the Fraternity's history thus far. Beginning in 1884, the <u>Quinquennial Catalogue,</u> the fifty year history of the Fraternity was published by the Fraternity's chapters. Included in this volume are historical sketches of each DU chapter through 1884, and a comprehensive list of membership; the book serving a dual purpose as an historical reference and member directory.

In 1934, the Fraternity published <u>Delta Upsilon, One Hundred Years</u>, which was written by Brother W. Freeman Galpin, *Northwestern '13*. Brother Galpin painstakingly recreated the history of the Fraternity, scars and all, in this volume, which was intended to be a true account of the history of the Fraternity, as opposed to a "song of praise". It is arguably one of the more detailed books of DU information through 1934, and reads much like a non-fiction novel.

Finally, in 1984, to celebrate the Fraternity's 150th Anniversary, the book <u>Challenge, Conflict and Change: The First 150 years of Delta Upsilon Fraternity</u> was written by Brother Orville H. Read, *Missouri '33*. This book was written as a "step by step" account of the Fraternity through its first one hundred fifty years, and served as a needed update to the Fraternity's comprehensive historical information.

<u>Revealing the Non-Secrets</u> is intended to be none of
that. No doubt that in 2034, the 200th Anniversary
history book will be produced, continuing the tradition
of an historical account every fifty years. The idea for
this book, however, came with a desire to produce
information that had, for the most part, not yet been
uncovered. It was written to simply celebrate the
Fraternity and its Founding, its rich history and
heritage. The book began, however, simply by divine
intervention.

Having always had a deep-rooted interest in history,
thanks to the influence of my paternal grandfather, I
was but minutes-old as a "pledge" of Delta Upsilon when
I inquired as to our Fraternity's history with the
question, "Who were our Founders?" Mark Hernandez,
Houston '92, my very capable Pledge Educator, informed
me that unfortunately there had been a fire in "the
1800s" at the Williams Chapter in which the records of
the early years of the Fraternity as well as the story of
the Founding had been destroyed. "We do not know
who our Founders were," it was stated. It was at that
very moment in time, when he finished his sentence,
that I pledged myself to find the answers. I said "before
I die, I am going to find out who our Founding Fathers
were, and piece our Founding story back together." On
that day, a love affair with Delta Upsilon Fraternity
began, and a figurative starter's pistol signaled the
beginning of what would become over a decade of part
time research.

For over ten years, this book was nagging at me from
the back of my mind, always reminding me that I had
an unquenchable desire to ensure that this story would
be recorded.

Over time, this love affair with Delta Upsilon would only intensify. Time would only help to strengthen my desire for the story to be uncovered, so that the memory and efforts of our Founders would be forever remembered. The sole purpose of this book is to ensure that the stance that these men took on November 4, 1834 would never be forgotten, and that future generations of Delta Upsilon would be able to benefit from a more in-depth account of the lives of our Fraternity's Founders.

The process of uncovering this information began in the late 1990s with the limited resources that I had at my disposal. It was not until the fall of 2000 that I was able to delve into the volumes of *Delta Upsilon Quarterly* magazines at the Delta Upsilon Headquarters in Indianapolis. Basic data was gleaned from these old issues, which led me to seek further biographical information from obituary records and other annals from the archives at Williams College. With information from another occasional book or two and the Internet, the majority of the details of the events and lives highlighted in this book began to come alive.

With every nugget of information I found, the more appalled I became that this information had not ever been compiled. I was excited to see our history come back together, but ashamed that we knew virtually nothing about our Founders and that we never had a solid historical account of our Founding. As my Delta Upsilon Brother Jeff Fuhrman, *Northern Iowa '94* so adeptly stated, "the lack of a known history mars the kinship we should feel with our first brothers."

As a result, this book is not so much a "175th History" of the Fraternity as it is an account and history of the Founding of Delta Upsilon and a tribute to the men who endured the scorn and ridicule of the secret fraternities at Williams, and persevered in their quest to create an alternative.

The answers, it turns out, were there all along. While the story of the "1800s fire" is true, the names of our founding brothers were very much known to us. There were actually two possible fires that affected the Fraternity at Williams, one more likely than the other. The Williams Chapter house caught fire in 1893 in what was then the second of the four houses that were ever occupied by the Williams Chapter of Delta Upsilon. The house burned, essentially leaving the four exterior walls intact. The house was rebuilt and still stands today on the corner of Southworth and Main Street in Williamstown, Massachusetts. No doubt some records were lost in that fire. But the Williams Chapter already had sixty years of history, which included a twenty-year period of dormancy. So the likelihood that early records would have burned in that fire is sketchy at best.

The more likely scenario, and one that is slightly backed up by a small clip of information in Fraternity records today, is a fire which occurred just seven years after the Founding. On Sunday, October 17, 1841, while the students were at church services, a fire broke out in the East College building, which was generally reserved for upperclassmen.

The older records of the Fraternity most likely would have been entrusted to an upperclassman officer, which at the time of the fire would have been the President, Vice-President or Corresponding Secretary, all of whom resided in East College that semester. So, it is extremely likely that the early records of the Social Fraternity were indeed lost in this 1841 fire.

The earliest known book to survive is the second minute book of the Social Fraternity which dates back to 1840. This book would have been in the hands of the Recording Secretary, James M. Wilson, *Williams 1844*. As a sophomore, Wilson would have resided in West College, which means the book that he would have been entrusted with would have stayed out of harm's way. The fact that this book survives helps to explain why the earlier records do not.

While I believe that we did indeed lose some important documents and official papers in that 1841 fire, I am not certain that we lost as much as was thought. Certainly, the names of our Founders survived the fire, as they have been documented over and over in past issues of *The Delta Upsilon Quarterly*, in the annals at Williams College, and in the various books in several remote locales in the United States.

The names were later carved into the mantle over the fireplace in the library of the last DU Chapter House at Williams, which still stands to this day. More importantly, they remained in the memory of the Founders themselves, who recounted those names in later years. The names of our Founders were also contained in Our Record, the member manual of Delta Upsilon prior to The Cornerstone.

Why they were not included in the latter reference remains a mystery to me.

Regardless, while the Fraternity did suffer an historical loss in the fire, the fact has also become an excuse to divert our attention away from the fact that our founding history and the lives of our Founders had never really been properly compiled or recorded.

The answers and many stories in this book were discovered with a rewarding information "treasure hunt". We discover through this pleasure trip, more than anything, a glimpse into the lives of our Founding Fathers. We discover much more than just their names. We discover who these men were, and the kind of character they possessed. Those who lived longer into maturity developed successful careers. Of all the Founders, twenty-one of them felt a calling to the ministry. Of the remaining nine we find a dentist, a family doctor, an engineer and a successful businessman. Another would serve as a newspaper publisher and Lieutenant Governor of a state, while another dedicated his life to education and would serve as the first President of the National Education Association. Finally, three judges would emerge, one of which served in what stands today as the second longest term of service on the United States Supreme Court. Despite their personal successes, we discover more than anything, that each and every one was a man of profound and sterling character. All of them were truly fine examples of what a Delta Upsilon man should be.

We have no secrets, only non-secrets. Yet for more than one hundred fifty years we have not told our story to anyone because those "non-secrets" had not been uncovered or revealed. In most cases, one reveals a secret. In this case, it is the non-secrets...

So with that, read on, and enjoy the information contained herein, as we are finally able to take part in "Revealing the Non-Secrets".

Craig S. Sowell, *Houston '92*
Fraternity Historian

Indianapolis, Indiana

The Thirty-First Founder?

Legend and tradition have always held that Delta Upsilon was founded by "thirty men, ten from each of the three lower classes". That fact or statement has always been accepted, perhaps out of the sheer convenience and symmetry of the legend.

However, after interviews with the then-surviving Founders who attended the Fraternity's Fiftieth Anniversary in 1884, it was suggested that there was indeed a thirty-first Founder. At that time, it was widely accepted that John H. Westfall, a member of the Freshman Class should be considered as one of the Fraternity's Founding Fathers. This would, of course, change the legend to "thirty-one men; ten from the junior and sophomore classes, and eleven from the freshman class".

Here, then, begins the difficulty. Research has been able to uncover a suitable glimpse into each of our Founder's lives, save for Brother Westfall. Not much on his life is known, nor could it be uncovered. The only significant facts about Brother Westfall's life have been that he hailed from Wantage Township, New Jersey and only attended Williams College from 1834 to 1836. Sometime after moving out of room number four in West College in 1836 he moved to either Georgia or to the western part of Virginia, which would eventually become the state of West Virginia. If the West Virginia John H. Westfall is "our John Westfall", then he married, became a farmer and fathered fourteen children. Certainly by 1891, as it was evidenced in the

Fraternity Catalogue of that year, Brother Westfall was deceased. It is believed that he likely died much earlier. The facts, however, are at this time unknown.

Not much is known about him or his fate after his departure from Williams soon after the Founding, which is largely why he may have fallen out of the focus of others as a Founder. We have no proof that he <u>was</u> present on that evening in November, other than the second hand report of the recorder at the Fiftieth Anniversary, who reported that the living Founders in 1884 all agreed Westfall was there that night. I suspect that because Westfall was his roommate in 1834, William Bross included Westfall among the list of Founders. A compelling argument, but unlike with the other thirty Founders, the fact of his presence there appears <u>nowhere</u> else, to my knowledge.

Though, we may never know that truth, Westfall is given mention in this author's note, so that he, too, will not be forgotten. However, because no information for him could be found and the evidence of his participation on that fateful night was not conclusive, the legend will live on as "thirty" Founders. And for the purposes of this book, I have used "thirty" as the reference.

C. Sowell

"Let nothing rob us of the spirit of Fraternity, let nothing destroy the bond of Delta Upsilon."

Charles Evans Hughes
Colgate & Brown 1881

Revealing the Non-Secrets

Introduction

The temperature would not have been so bad if it were not for the brisk wind that also swirled the leaves on the ground. Were it not for the wind, it would have still felt like autumn, but it was clear that winter was already on its way. An ungloved hand was nearly frozen with just three minutes exposure to the cold wind. As the sun was closing its eyelid on the horizon, dusk fell upon the campus of Williams College, nestled in the tiny hamlet of Williamstown, Massachusetts, in the shadows of the Berkshires.

The campus was eerily silent this night as most of the one hundred and nineteen students were already snug in their rooms and reading <u>Hedge's Logic</u>, Homer's <u>The Iliad</u> or practicing their lessons for the following day from <u>Day's Logarithms</u>.

Thirty of these students, however, were making their final preparations for a meeting. A scant handful had arrived early to help set the room, light some oil lamps, and prepare a fire in the hearth to scare the chill out of the room. Ten men, all juniors, were donning their coats and gloves to brave the brisk night air for the short walk across campus to the West College building from their rooms in East College.

The rest of the men, all of whom resided in West College, were beginning to make their way down the hall, or either up or down stairs to the second floor Freshman Recitation Room.

15

The room was used during the day for many purposes, not the least of which was a daily "chapel" for the sophomore and freshman students. The room would also provide a suitable place for what was about to occur. A birth – a beginning was about to take place, and this room would unknowingly seal its immortality and become the hallowed halls of a Founding...

The Founding

The Founding

1834. It was in the historical time period in the early
United States known as the Westward Expansion.
Although Lewis and Clark had completed their travels
almost thirty years before, the western frontier had not
yet stretched beyond the Mississippi River. Many
families were still living in log cabins or in covered
wagons filled with all of their possessions as they
headed west to find their fortunes. Things were a little
more sophisticated on the east coast, however. After all,
over two hundred years of progress had been made since
the founding of Jamestown in 1607. Brick homes were
common in metropolitan areas like Philadelphia and
New York City, both of which bustled with activity.

President Andrew Jackson, who had been elected to a
second term in 1832, was still reeling from being
censured by the United State Senate for his actions in
de-funding the Second Bank of the United States, while
a twenty-five year old Abraham Lincoln began his
political career by being elected to his first term in the
Illinois House of Representatives. In June, the United
States Congress created the "Indian Territory" (mainly
in present-day Oklahoma) as a homeland for forcibly
displaced Native Americans, and the United States
made its way westward, with all land west of the
Mississippi River still largely considered wild and
untamed.

Headlines for the year included Cyrus McCormick's
patent for the reaping machine, the completion of the
first railroad tunnel in the United States; adhesive

postage stamps and the game of poker made their debut, and Isaac Fischer, Jr., of Springfield, Vermont received the U.S. patent for making sandpaper. Delmonico's, one of New York's finest restaurants, advertised a meal of soup, steak, coffee and half a pie for twelve cents. Long pants, which replaced knee breeches, had only been in vogue for about twenty years. The United States of America, twenty-four in all, had just celebrated fifty-five years of existence and was preparing to mark the thirty-fifth anniversary of the death of President George Washington.

Mark Twain's birth was still one year away, and the Battle of the Alamo and Texas' Independence from Mexico would not be settled for another eighteen months. It was a three-year wait for the invention of the telegraph. The beginning of the reign of Britain's Queen Victoria and the legendary "discovery" of modern day baseball in America would be another five years away. Even Thomas Edison's light bulb was not even a thought, as Edison himself would not be "invented" for another twelve years.

There was no electricity in homes of course, and people would have to wait another fifty years before running water or indoor plumbing would even begin to become commonplace. Getting a drink of water in winter meant putting on a full armor of winter clothing and stepping outside to the water pump with the hopes that the pump was not iced over. Taking a bath meant drawing water once a week and heating it on a stove before putting it in the tub. A full day of travel might consist of twenty miles if one was pulling a wagon.

Life in the eastern United States was still much more advanced than for those who ventured west, but the times were still simple and primitive compared to modern day.

Life was seemingly simpler still for the college student. In this day and time, it was mostly the male gender that had the option to attend college, but few had the opportunity. For starters, distance made it impossible for some to attend. For others, it was the financial burden, with few families able to afford the tuition. At Williams that fee could be as much as twelve dollars per semester! For most boys of college age, the reason for not attending was simple – they were <u>also</u> of age to carry their weight at home on the farm, in the fields, or tending to the family business and learning their trade.

For those fortunate enough to attend college in the early 1800s, most of them understood that it was a <u>privilege</u> to attend. Those who enrolled showed promise of intellect and adhered to the highest standard of personal discipline. To succeed in college, a student invested a large amount of time on his own reading volume upon volume of literature. Time had to be spent in his room practicing lessons of logic and mathematical logarithms, studying ancient languages, philosophy, natural history and theology.

Exercise came naturally, as the main method of transportation was on foot. One might walk several miles a day without even trying. Walking to the edge of town or even to the next town and back would give the student more than enough exercise. Some students even had the opportunity to work during their off time, mainly in the fields or on the farmland.

This work provided them a meager wage certainly, but many took advantage of the work for the recreation and exercise it provided.

Williams College, founded in 1793, was the second college established in the state of Massachusetts after Harvard University. One might wonder why the choice was made to form a college in the tiny northwestern corner of the state. The reasoning was recorded in the minutes of the founding Trustees of the college. The location offered some compelling points, not the least of which was to provide a more affordable solution for students. Affordability enticed more middle to lower income level students who would not otherwise have the opportunity to attend college. Being in a remote location and surrounded by mountains, there would also be less opportunity for distraction and temptation, allowing the students a stronger academic focus. The location would also allow the college to draw potential students from neighboring Vermont, New Hampshire, New York and Connecticut.

By 1834, Williams College had already established a fine forty-year reputation for preparing its students for life's adventures. Courses taught at Williams included Mathematics, Natural Philosophy,[1] Theology, Ancient Languages, Moral and Intellectual Philosophy, English Language and Literature and Natural History. The faculty at Williams numbered five in all, including the well-respected and admired Dr. Mark Hopkins, who would later serve as President of the College.

---

[1] Natural Philosophy was the study of nature and the universe prior to the development of modern science. Natural Philosophy would equate more closely today as Physics or Physical Science.

There was but five buildings on campus and a professor-to-student ratio of one for every twenty-five students. In this day and time, college was a year-round effort with students attending during the summer as usual occurrence.

Sketch by E.B. and F.C. Kellogg depicting the
Williams College campus in about 1830.
West College is the larger building on the left between the trees

Image courtesy of Williams College Archives and Special Collections

1834 was also a time of religious revival in America. When not studying other lessons or conducting hour upon hour of memorization in classes, students were expected to also devote time to their daily devotion, Bible reading and quiet time. Even more, students were expected to awaken before sunrise for individual prayer time and the same again at sunset. At Williams there was a higher expectation of this practice, as the college was known for preparing students who aspired to a career in the ministry. Even the Williams College President, Dr. Edward Dorr Griffin, doubled as the professor of theology. It is a known fact that of the Fraternity's thirty founding members, twenty-one of them pursued a career in ministry.

West College, a simple but stately federal-style building that had been constructed in 1790, was the first building on the Williams campus when the school began in 1793. In fact, for the first four years of the college, the West College building was Williams College. It was the lone building of the school until, by the time of the Founding in 1834, the campus had expanded to five buildings. It lacked all of the modern conveniences of electricity, plumbing and water, but was well-built, strong and formidable. It was built upon a hill of limestone that overlooked Williamstown and was resistant to well digging. As a result the students had to trek down a quarter mile wooded path just southwest of the building, diagonally across what was then known as "Deacon Skinner's Meadow," to retrieve their water from a spring, known as "Walden Spring" or the "College Spring".

The West College building was originally constructed to accommodate one hundred students. By 1834, it was reserved as a dormitory for freshmen and sophomores. It had a broad hallway that ran from east to west that divided the building, with both the east and west doorways opening to a double-staircase to the second floor. From the second to the third and the third to the fourth floors, there was but one staircase each on the south end of the east-west hallway.

24

When it was originally completed in 1790, West College's four floors contained all that a student would need. The fourth floor contained nothing but student dorm rooms, each complete with a bed, desk, chair, chiffarobe,[2] and a stove for winter heat. The first floor contained classrooms on the north half, and a dining area and kitchen on the south half. The second and third floors, likewise, contained dorm rooms on the north half of the building. On the south half of the building there was no floor between the second and third floors. This created a large, open, two-story room south half of the second floor, known as the Chapel. It primarily served as a daily chapel for the students and could be used for various meetings, commencement exercises and other important events.

The upper half of the room boasted a gallery on either end that was accessible from the third floor. Each gallery would have run the length of the room and been about six to eight feet wide, deep enough for people to sit "two-deep" and still have room to spare for an aisle in between. Overflow audiences would have sat in the gallery to view the orations, commencement exercises, etc.

The lower half of the room was accessible from the second floor. On the west wall was a stage with a desk upon it, and elevated seats that were primarily used by the professors and tutors. The students would sit in long wooden benches in the center of the main floor to the eastern wall.

---

[2] A chiffarobe is a freestanding wardrobe containing drawers and a rod for hanging clothes with a full length mirror on the door. It is similar to an armoire but slightly smaller.

Sketch by Edward Valois depicting
West College in about 1790

Image courtesy of Williams College Archives and Special Collections

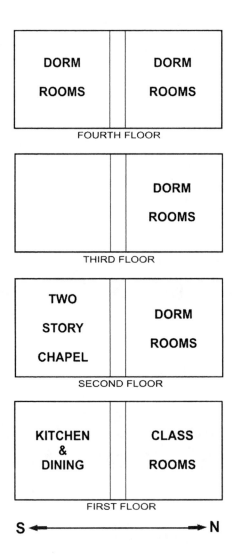

West College floor plan: 1790 – 1828.

In 1828, the completion of Griffin Hall included a new Chapel on the ground floor. This expansion allowed for a remodel of West College. It was in 1828 when a floor was constructed in West College to "fill in" the third floor of the south end of the building, essentially cutting the old two-story chapel room in half. This conversion created separate and specific "recitation rooms" for each of the sophomore and freshmen classes. The new third floor room was designated as the Sophomore Recitation Room, with the second floor room becoming the Freshman Recitation Room.

The Freshman Recitation Room would have been built in the same style as the lower half of the room shown above. The area to the left of the fireplace, where the chairs are lined up below the windows, would have held a stage area where the orations would have been conducted, etc.

During this time period, college students at Williams did not take paper examinations. All exams were conducted orally in front of a single professor. Students would prepare to recite their newly acquired knowledge in the form of an oration performed in the presence of the professor, who then graded the students on their presentation and their fluency of subject knowledge.

The Freshman Recitation Room[3] provided a suitable place where freshmen could practice their orations in front of upperclassmen who would provide welcome feedback and instruction before the underclassmen performed their oration formally in front of the professor the next day.

In 1847, the construction of Kellogg Hall allowed for two new recitation rooms, which became the new home for the freshman and sophomore recitations. At this time, the recitation rooms, kitchen and dining area were removed from West College. West College was then converted to house only dormitory rooms.

Fraternities at Williams first made an appearance in 1833, just a year before Delta Upsilon made its mark. Kappa Alpha Society, the first social fraternity founded in America, was the first to arrive at Williams when a group of students took a "road trip" to Union College for the purpose of returning with a charter of Phi Beta

---

[3] The Freshman Recitation Room that became the birthplace of the Social Fraternity existed only from 1828 to 1847. Although no photos of the recitation room are known to exist, one can get an idea of what the room looked like by viewing the lower half of the chapel room in Griffin Hall today in the photo at left.

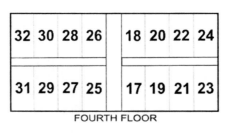

| 32 30 28 26 | 18 20 22 24 |
| 31 29 27 25 | 17 19 21 23 |

FOURTH FLOOR

| SOPHOMORE RECITATION ROOM | 10 12 14 16 |
| | 9 11 13 15 |

THIRD FLOOR

| FRESHMAN RECITATION ROOM | 2 4 6 8 |
| | 1 3 5 7 |

SECOND FLOOR

| KITCHEN & DINING | CLASS ROOMS |

FIRST FLOOR

West College floor plan: 1828 – 1847
Room numbering is author's calculated
guess based on factual information.

Kappa, of which Williams College president, Dr. Edward Dorr Griffin had been a member at Yale University. Their quest went unfulfilled, however, because Union College was in New York and thus did not have jurisdiction to establish a charter at a school in a different state. Williams College was, of course, in Massachusetts. The group, instead, returned with a charter establishing themselves as a chapter of Kappa Alpha Society. Dr. Griffin welcomed the new group even though they were not Phi Beta Kappa. He recognized though, that there was indeed a "Kappa" within the keys (badges) they had received, so he naturally assumed it was a favorable association and supported the effort.

Shortly after the arrival of Kappa Alpha, the Sigma Phi Fraternity established a chapter at Williams as well. These two fraternities set about providing a social respite from the rigors of daily classroom memorization and study time. Some suggest that the fraternities provided additional intellectual stimulation, which is in part, true. However, the main purpose of their formation was for pure social interaction and to provide a familial atmosphere for the students, who were away from home and secluded in the little Berkshire hamlet of Williamstown.

Even before the 1833 founding of fraternities at Williams, a society already existed called the "Adelphic Union," which served as a debate and literary society. Within five short years of the founding of the college, the Union had split into two separate societies, the Philologian and the Philotechnian Societies, thanks to continuous and growing interest in their activities.

Upon entering college, a student was assigned to one of these two societies for their literary improvement.

Truth be told, the two secret fraternities that had been established at Williams allowed the Philologian and Philotechnian societies to be the intellectual outlets, while they themselves became the full social escape for the students. Yes, even in 1833, the secret fraternities became "boys' clubs" where smoking, card playing and drinking were the norm. Students even then were known to smuggle hard cider, wine, dark ale or other spirits into their room for "safe keeping". And, while the establishment of fraternities did nothing to slow the intensity of the religious revival that was still growing at that time, they did indeed begin to lessen the intensity of some students' desires to enter into ministerial careers. This was a possible threat to the reputation of Williams College, known for producing such devout clergymen. Students, who were once faithful in their evening prayer time, were now forgoing the more reverent activities for those more irreverent. The fraternities began to represent and foster a lack of unity among the students and the religious community.

By late October of 1834, enrollment for classes in the winter quarter was complete. The campus possessed a seemingly congenial attitude among the students, but blood was already boiling in the veins of some of the members of the sophomore and junior classes. For several years prior, members of the two fraternities on campus, despite their reputation among the student body as "clubhouses", had monopolized the control of student affairs on campus and held all of the offices and leadership roles in the literary societies. Their influence was felt, and was decidedly nothing short of overbearing and oppressive to non-members. Although these fraternities had existed for more than a year, the faculty had hardly taken notice of their activities, but the students certainly had.

In fact, mannerisms of the fraternity men became a divisive force to some. In one particular instance, early one morning while the students were assembled for a recitation, the door of the classroom was opened and a number of young men filed slowly into the classroom, displaying the golden key of the Kappa Alpha Society pinned on the left chest of their shirts. A pause was made at once in the recitation while the men entered, and many students who witnessed it were sickened by the air of conceit and arrogance.

Francis Tappan was one of those students whose stomach turned at the negative atmosphere that was developing on the campus as a result of the attitude of these fraternity men. He and a different group of students decided to take a similar but subtle action to show their disapproval. A few mornings after the display of fraternity arrogance, Tappan and this group of students, nearly equal in number as before, walked into the room with the same deliberation as the fraternity men had. They each wore bright brass inscriptionless triangles pinned to their shirts. Tappan would later write that *"consternation was manifest in the countenances of the members of the two secret societies, who wore their breast pins and keys, and not a word was spoken. By agreement previously made, no person was to be permitted to handle our triangles or examine for their letterings, for there were no inscriptions. No organization had adopted them; they were not Badges and had no signification, but were empty brass."*

The students had succeeded in making their disapproval known, but had also mocked the ridiculousness of the secret fraternities and what they stood for, or in fact, did not stand for. In doing so, they had also poked at the proverbial hornet's nest of the fraternities. In a way they were becoming themselves, the very thing they despised – a selective clique. Still the benefits outweighed the negatives, they thought, and the tension between the two factions continued to mount.

In addition to Tappan, there was another sophomore who was becoming equally dissatisfied. During his undergraduate days at Williams, Stephen Johnson Field was "passed up" for election to the student government. Legend has it that Field was either not considered for election or lost an election for student government by virtue of the fact that he was an "independent", meaning he did not belong to one of the secret fraternities that held the balance of power in the college. The thought infuriated the tenacious young Field, who decided that a change was in order. Already the secret societies were ruining the very Christian fabric of the college by their mere existence. In addition, he also recognized a need for a college literary organization of fewer and more closely knit members and of broader scope than the Philologian and Philotechnian societies, but also of deeper meaning than the secret fraternities. This thought, coupled with the most recent oppressive and exclusive measure encountered by Field was the final straw.

Never one to sit idly by, Field had to talk to someone about his frustration and began a conversation one morning with his fellow classmate Tappan, who was equally fed up with the "tainted fabric" of student leadership. Tappan and Field both knew others of their class who felt the same way, causing Tappan to suggest a meeting in his room that evening to propose a plan of action. After dinner that night, Field and fellow sophomore, Lewis Lockwood, trekked over to East College to meet with Tappan in his room. It was in Room Twenty-Two where they all agreed that it was time for a change. However, they also agreed that the sophomores alone would not be able to make a significant impact unless they had at least some measure of support from some of the upperclassmen. This was not some sophomoric club that they were proposing. Instead they envisioned a global change to the atmosphere of the student body of Williams College. Together they devised a simple recruitment plan. They would not post flyers on campus, nor would an article appear in any campus publication, nor announcement be made during mealtime or chapel services. This would be a grass roots effort of conducting one-on-one conversations with individuals in their rooms. And, in some cases, they would catch the ear of a pair of roommates and sign on "two for the price of one."

Tappan found great success in first securing ten members of the junior class who agreed a change was needed. While they were not long for their time in college, they were still drawn by their moral conviction to fulfill a need within the Williams campus culture, and leave their alma mater better than they found it. During this time, Field and Lockwood were also having great success in West College, with Tappan also assisting in the underclassman effort. While Tappan was the only <u>true</u> underclassman that resided in East College with the juniors and seniors, he would make his trek to West College daily for study with his sophomore classmates, and he knew them all well. Together, Tappan and Field first and very wisely targeted William Bross, a bright young freshman. Bross lived on the same small section on the second floor where seven of the ten freshman revolutionaries lived. Bross was not only an extrovert, but a true leader that exuded the necessary qualities that would help influence others and help bolster a fledgling group. People were naturally drawn to Bross. If they could just get Bross to "sign on", then it was natural that others would follow as a matter of course.

Considering that the secret fraternity actions were "ruining the Christian fabric" of the campus, it was only natural that those students who were studying for a career in the ministry would be sympathetic to a cause that would help strengthen and bolster that very fabric. Students like Bross, while not studying for a full time ministerial career, still held to deeply rooted religious beliefs, which made them a perfect addition to the group of patriots. Tappan and Lockwood, with some assistance from Stephen Field, took Bross aside to explain their vision, and their plan. Bross was not only immediately sympathetic to the reasoning behind the plan, but was eager to be a part of it.

For the next few days, they continued discussions with several other men. They would have late night conversations with their roommates. Converts would beget converts. They would discuss the very idea at a private lunch table; they would have one-on-one

36

discussions while walking the road to North Adams and back as part of their daily exercise routine; they would retreat to collect a pail of water from the stream, but would take their time for the purposes of having an important discussion. Through all of these discussions, a commitment was secured from each of the recruits to attend a group meeting that was planned for the following Tuesday night. Their recruitment efforts had resulted in the individual commitments of thirty men, very uniformly made up from ten of each of the three lower classes. There, they would collectively discuss their plan for organizing a revolt, not with the intent of starting a fight, but with the intent of raising awareness of their dissatisfaction. The purpose of the new society, they decided, would be for the maintenance of social equality, peaceful conduct and high moral principles. Their intent was a peaceful and intellectual revolt, but the result would be perceived by the secret societies as a "frontal attack".

Tuesday, November Fourth, and the day of their proposed meeting had arrived. The cloudy day had yielded an ironic temperature of thirty-four degrees at dusk. The campus population went about their daily activities as usual, but each of the thirty men were mentally preparing for the important meeting later that evening, many of them spending time in fervent prayer for what was to come.

After dinner that evening, the sun was closing in on the horizon, and dusk fell upon the campus of Williams College. What little sun had been out on this cloudy day was now gone. The cold temperature would not have been so bad were it not for the brisk wind that swirled the leaves on the ground and chilled the bones of the students. Were it not for the wind, it would have still felt like fall, but it was clear that winter was already on its way.

The campus itself was eerily silent this night as most of the one hundred and nineteen students were already in their rooms reading, studying or practicing their lessons for the following day by the light of oil lamps.

Thirty of these students, however, were making their final preparations. A scant handful had arrived early to help set the room, light some oil lamps, and prepare a fire in the hearth to scare the chill out of the room. Ten men, all juniors, were collectively donning their coats and gloves to brave the brisk night air for the short walk across campus to the West College building from their rooms in East College. The remaining men, all of whom resided in West College, were beginning to make their way down the hall, or either up or down stairs to the second floor.

At the appointed time, the meeting would quietly begin. There would be no rap of a gavel, nor a sound of trumpets, nor a paraded entrance of officers. The meeting would simply begin, with thirty men of character calmly and patiently sitting, listening and debating the issues together. Francis Tappan, Stephen Field and Lewis Lockwood would highlight the discussions held days before in Room Twenty-Two of East College, and the thoughts that had occupied their minds and subsequently prompted that meeting.

They would present the fact that the campus of Williams College was in desperate need of leadership from men of character; right minded, level headed, strong willed men of character. Not only were the secret fraternities in reckless control, but they were fighting amongst themselves, which certainly did not set the tone nor the example for the students of the campus. The tenor was so severe that many of the students who were rival fraternity members were not on speaking terms with each other. There was neither time nor room for any affable sentiment such as "Can't we all just get along?" Something had to be done, and that something fell upon the shoulders of this band of men who now met this night.

"It would not be easy," Field would say. "We may very well be starting a revolution of sorts. We will experience contempt and ridicule. We will feel the effects of scorn and opposition, but it must be done. If any of you are not one with us in our principles or do not believe in our purpose, you are free to exit this room with no fear of ridicule from us whatsoever." They waited. The only sound that could be heard at that point, was the deafening sound…of silence. No one moved. No one exited. Their silence and the utterance of not one single word spoke volumes.

"Very well then," Field continued, "tonight we will band together, to prove to the student body, to Williams College, to God and to ourselves, that we are men of strong character and that we desire to right the wrongs on this campus and be steadfast in our efforts. Our society will be founded upon principles which appeal to the higher and nobler nature of man, quietly pursuing the even tenor of its way, not only holding its own, but steadily increasing in strength and influence."

They called their new society, The Social Fraternity.

That night, they held the first election and selected the Social Fraternity's first President, Anson Hobart, a junior who was destined to become a doctor of medicine. Hobart was well-liked among the juniors and easily won the confidence of the freshmen and sophomores as well. He looked like a leader and acted like a leader. He had both a steady hand and mind, and was not one to waver or make a decision without first carefully thinking about the consequences of that decision. He was a calming influence, yet dedicated to the cause. He was, by all accounts, a natural choice to lead the group into being.

The group also formed a committee of two, Daniel Brown and Edward Clarke, to begin authoring the first constitution of the society,[4] and then adjourned the meeting and prepared themselves for the next day. Their collective prophesy was correct. They did indeed endure the scorn that they had foretold, as Founder William Bross would recollect just a few years later in a letter to the Williams Chapter on the tenth anniversary of the Founding:

"The Society was formed on the evening of November 4, 1834. Some disturbance occurred the next day on account of the formation of our Society. The secret societies endeavored to ridicule us. Badges of every description of caricature were worn by them. Classic epithets were given to us. We bore this patiently and fearlessly; and often did the advocates of the secret societies find that there were blows to take as well as blows to give. But, these were the blows of honorable intellectual effort. The Principles of the Fraternity being open and correct, it needed not the aid of ridicule or

---

[4] See Appendix for the Preamble and Constitution of the early Society.

anything low and groveling to sustain it. Appealing to the brighter and the nobler principles of man's intellectual and moral nature, its course was onward and upward."

Because of the soundness of the new Social Fraternity's principles and the moral character of its members, it grew to the point that within two years, the membership boasted eighty-two members, nearly two-thirds of the entire student population of Williams College.

Within four years, the same sentiment was felt, which resulted in a similar effort just a few miles away at Union College in Schenectady, New York. By 1840, just six short years after the Founding at Williams, the non-secret group at Union sought affiliation with the Williams Chapter. By 1847, the groups at Williams and Union were joined by similar groups at Amherst and Hamilton Colleges. Together, they met at what was deemed as the organization's first convention and created the Anti-Secret Confederation. In August of 1858, the Anti-Secret Confederation had grown to seven active chapters, which together, officially adopted "Delta Upsilon" as the name for the organization.

Over the next one-hundred-fifty years, what began as a formal stance on principle by a band of thirty men would grow and expand to more than one-hundred-fifty chapters across the United States and Canada, accepting more than 125,000 men into its fold.

West College, still stately after 200 years...

Photo taken November 4, 2004

The Founders

The Founders

The pages that follow are not intended to tell a story. They are intended to create a collective historical record; an account of the lives of thirty individuals that came together to form the first non-secret fraternity. They are not unlike any of us today in many ways. They recruited their friends. They recruited their roommates. They were true to themselves, and to each other.

Many of the lives that are recorded on the following pages look very similar on the surface. Each of them was a true man of sound character, which is very evident in their stories. Twenty-one of the thirty entered a career in religion and ministry. Reading their individual stories, one might think that one is the same as the next. They are all here for the simple reason that they started a fraternity together.

The truth is that each of these men led very individual lives. Each of them, obviously, had unique traits and personalities. Each of them came to their life choices by traversing down a unique path. Each of them had their own personal reasons for deciding to take a stand on November 4, 1834. Those individual reasons we may never uncover. Regardless, we are fortunate to have glimpses, whether long or short, into each of their lives. Their legacy lives on today in the continuation of Delta Upsilon, but at last, now, their stories may finally be told.

45

The Class of 1836

Algernon Sidney Baldwin

Hiram Bell

George Clisby

Samuel Dana Darling

Anson Loomis Hobart

Ephraim William Kellogg

Josiah Lyman

Lebbeus Rude Phillips

Zalmon Richards

Edmund Wright

The Juniors

The class of 1836, or "the first ten of one of the three lower classes" at Williams in November of 1834, was arguably the most engaged of any of the classes in terms of school spirit. While the clear majority of the Founders had an affinity for Williams College later in life, this group clearly shines brighter than the rest. First, they are the only one of the three classes of Founders to boast a one-hundred percent graduation rate. That is to say that all of the ten Founders from the junior class graduated from Williams. It is not surprising then, that many of them would return for their Williams class reunions in their later years. Thanks to the photographs collected at these reunions, more photos of the class of 1836 exist than for any other class.

All of them were well-established in their own right. Eight of the ten studied to be in the ministry, including two that died early in life. Those who lived did so well into the 1870s and beyond. The two who did not pursue a ministerial direction still held to their religious beliefs, but chose to pursue careers in medicine and education instead.

At Williams, these ten were the men who would provide the first leadership and stable direction for the Fraternity. They were the rudder of the ship that steered the early voyage of non-secrecy. In this class are found the first and second presidents of the Social Fraternity, and essentially, the first Recruitment Chairman. In terms of academics, they were also the men who would provide the scholarly direction to the members of the sophomore and freshman classes, and give them feedback and tutelage for their education.

Without the junior class, the Founding of Delta Upsilon is nothing more than an uprising of disgruntled "sprouts" of underclassmen. They would, essentially, bring the necessary credibility to the new effort with a strong showing of upper-class support.

To boil it all down, these men would be the "big brothers" for the new group of fraternity men …

ALGERNON SIDNEY BALDWIN '36
"The Introvert"

Born:	March 2, 1811
Died:	September 30, 1839 (age 28)
Buried:	Water Street Cemetery
	Great Barrington, Massachusetts
Marriage:	None
Children:	None
Occupation:	Theological Student
Dorm Room:	19 East College

Originally thought to have been born in 1807, Algernon Sidney Baldwin was actually born on March 2, 1811 in Great Barrington, Massachusetts to Davis and Amy Baldwin. He spent the early years of his life growing up in Tyringham, Massachusetts with his parents and three younger brothers, Irwin, Edmund and Orrin. Although the oldest of four brothers, in his boyhood he was feeble, sickly and likely suffered from asthma.

When he was sixteen years of age, he made a public confession of faith and united himself with the Congregational Church in Tyringham. Convinced of his future, he began working towards his vocation as a minister.

At the age of eighteen, he moved to Lenox, Massachusetts and entered the Lenox Academy where he prepared for college. While at Lenox, he found a job as a public school teacher to help pay his own tuition, room and board, accepting no financial assistance from others.

Lenox Academy – Lenox, MA

He studied at Lenox for three years before deciding the time was right to attend college. Soon after turning twenty-one, he enrolled at Williams College.
His classmates remember him as "tall and cadaverous looking, slow of speech and somewhat awkward in manner, but maintained an honorable reputation as a hard student, a genial and interesting companion."[5] He was a voracious reader, and was known for having a large stock of general knowledge on a variety of subjects.

Initiating a self-imposed vow of poverty, to save money and so as to not inconvenience others, he refused to indulge in certain luxuries of which a normal person might have taken advantage.

---

[5] From the Williams College Biographical Annals

Rather than riding in a carriage when he visited home from college, for example, he chose to walk instead, even though the distance was about thirty-seven miles!

A self-proclaimed loner, he much preferred to spend time alone, almost enjoying his indigent circumstances and relishing the opportunity to read rather than to be out among the masses. In this time period, it was not common for people of his age to be so inclined to seclusion. Even so, he did enjoy visiting with people with whom he was familiar, and he would meet with them for long periods at a time, even lecturing them on various subjects, including temperance, of which he was a strong advocate.

After graduating from Williams in 1836, he moved to Great Barrington, Massachusetts, where his health began to decline. It was almost as if he expected this fate, as he had surprisingly held off his professional studies, even the seminary, while hoping and waiting for his health to return.

In the summer of 1838, he experienced severe bleeding from his lungs and was forced to stop all of his activities. He accepted his inevitable fate "with a submissive spirit", and retained all of his mental faculties until the very end.

On September 30, 1839, just three short years after graduating from Williams, he died at the age of twenty-eight; a victim of tuberculosis. He was "very highly esteemed at the time of his death, which was greatly lamented by the people where he had spent most of his life."[6] He was buried in the family plot in Water Street Cemetery in the town where he was born.

---

[6] From the <u>Williams College Biographical Annals</u>

REV. HIRAM BELL '36
"The Benevolent One"

Born: December 16, 1807
Died: June 18, 1876 (age 68)
Buried: Westchester Cemetery
                    Colchester, Connecticut
Marriage: July 1, 1840
                    Mary E. Wells (d. 1/22/1897)
Children: Five
Occupation: Minister
Dorm Room: 23 East College

Not much is known about the family or early life of
Hiram Bell of New Hampshire. He was born in the
town of Antrim on December 16, 1807. At the turn of
the nineteenth century, Antrim was a small quiet town
dotted with saw mills, grist mills and silk mills, thanks
to the strong stream that ran through town – a great
advantage to mills and factories. This is where Hiram
Bell grew up and worked on his family farm until he
was seventeen years old.

He soon grew tired of farm life and yearned for other
fulfillment. In 1824, he moved to Boston and for the
next four years he lived there and worked as a store
clerk. In 1828, he moved back to New Hampshire to
prepare for college at Kimball Academy,[7] a college
preparatory school in Meriden. After graduating from
Kimball, and having earned a reputation for being a
good scholar and strong Christian, he enrolled in

---

[7] Now Kimball Union Academy

Hiram Bell
Williams 1836

*Image courtesy of Williams College
Archives and Special Collections*

Williams College in 1832 to pursue an education in the field of religion.

He was very cordial and sympathetic, a good companion, and well-liked by his fellow students. His classmates remembered him as being calm and serious in his demeanor, and stable and consistent in his actions. While not considered "brilliant," he certainly showed that he was a good, serious and dedicated student and a judicious worker.

In his junior year he was stricken with a high fever and was near death. His classmates, however, looked after him, happily volunteering their services when they were called upon, for which Bell would express his gratitude in later years saying that "his life had been saved by their kind attentions." Graduating with a fair reputation as a scholar and Christian, he studied theology and completed the three-year course at the seminary in East Windsor, Connecticut,[8] where he would later serve as a Trustee for many years. He was an upstanding individual and very well thought of at seminary as well. A fellow student once wrote of him saying, "He was a sound preacher, of mature and settled convictions, and a good speaker. He was a good pastor and preacher and well-liked by all to whom he ministered." He took an active role in campus discussions and ministerial societies while at the seminary, and "stood well with his brethren in the ministry and with the churches."

On Feb. 19, 1840 he was ordained as a pastor at a church in Marlboro, Connecticut, where he preached for

---

[8] Now Hartford Seminary in Hartford, Connecticut

ten years. On July 1, 1840, he married Miss Mary Wells of Sing Sing, New York.

On December 23, 1841, they welcomed their first child, Edward Wells Bell. Nearly two years later, they experienced both joy and pain when their daughter Mary Jane was born on September 4, 1843, dying later that same day. Four years later, on that exact day, they welcomed daughter Sarah Elizabeth, making September 4 a bittersweet date for the Bell family. Another son, Charles Hiram, joined them on April 4, 1849.

In November 1850, Pastor Bell was installed over the church in Killingworth, Connecticut, where he remained for fourteen years, when failing health forced him to slow down his activities. During his time there, he again experienced both joy and sadness. With his wife Mary eight months pregnant with their fifth child, their daughter Sarah passed away on August 19, 1852, just a couple of weeks before her fifth birthday. Just a month later that sadness was likely buffered with the joyous addition of their third son, Albert Wells Bell, who joined the family on September 10, 1852.

Moving again in June of 1864, the Bell family settled in Westchester, a parish in the town of Colchester, where he lived, preached and enjoyed his new granddaughter Francis, born to youngest son Albert on June 18, 1875.

Hiram would only enjoy the role of grandfather for a short time, however. He developed an abscess of the liver, which caused him great discomfort and progressively worsened. As the family rejoiced in his granddaughter's first birthday on June 18, 1876, Hiram Bell died calmly and peacefully at the age of 68 with his family at his side. While he was deprived of robust strength and health in his later years he was satisfied with the life that he had led.

He was buried in the family plot in Westchester Cemetery, just down the lane from the church where he preached.

GEORGE CLISBY '36
"The Prodigy"

Born: August 26, 1816
Died: October 24, 1836 (age 20)
Buried: Salem Street Burial Ground
                     Medford, MA
Marriage: None
Children: None
Occupation: Theological Student
Dorm Room: 29 East College

A native of Medford, Massachusetts, George Clisby was one of the youngest and most promising of the Class of 1836. Unfortunately, he was also the first of the Founders to pass into "Chapter Eternal", in some way becoming "Delta Upsilon's first alumnus."

He was born on August 25, 1816 in Medford, where he spent his formative years. A very bright boy, he entered Williams College in 1832 at the age of sixteen. In the class record he is spoken of as "being a truly consistent Christian, and standing high as a scholar, having a discriminative and cultivated mind and an unusual share of general knowledge."[9] He also would have been the one to most likely be elected "most handsome" by his entire class of 1836, had such elections taken place. George Clisby was the "whole package." At Williams he was in good company, sharing Room Twenty-Nine with Anson Hobart of New Hampshire, who would later serve as the fledgling fraternity's first president.

_____

[9] From the <u>Williams College Biographical Annals</u>

61

In August of 1836, he graduated from Williams College and moved back temporarily to Medford, where he was focused on pursuing a life in Christian ministry and looking forward to, if so directed, a life in the field as a missionary. He was preparing to enter the seminary at Andover, Massachusetts[10] when he became very ill. He had contracted Typhus,[11] likely through the bite of a flea or tick. On October 24, 1836, just two months after graduating from Williams, George Clisby passed away at the age of twenty and was buried in the Salem Street Burial Ground in Medford, Massachusetts.

Highly revered by his peers, upon his death the class secretary of 1836 wrote in regard to "his piety and his prospects for eternity, may the last end of each individual of the class be like his." Clearly a standout and promising new alumnus of Williams, his death was obviously felt by the entire college. For a man whose looks, character and intellect could bring him virtually anything he wanted, he remained sincere and pious to the very end. There was nothing fake about George Clisby.

The faculty and even the students who remained behind at the college, took up a collection to install a white marble monument over his grave. Time and weather have smoothed the engraved tablet beyond recognition, but thanks to good historical archives, we have a record of the following inscription:

---

[10] Now Andover Newton Theological Seminary
[11] Different from Typhoid Fever

In memory of
GEORGE CLISBY
Who died Oct. 24, 1836
Aged 20 Years.

*In testimony of their respect
for him as a scholar, and an
affectionate remembrance of
his amiable character and
Christian virtues, this stone
is erected by the officers and
students of Williams College,
at which institution he
graduated a few weeks
previous to his death.*

Samuel Dana Darling
Williams 1836

*Image courtesy of Williams College
Archives and Special Collections*

REV. SAMUEL DANA DARLING '36
"The Strong One"

Born:	February 7, 1807
Died:	May 5, 1873 (Age 66)
Buried:	Avoca Cemetery
	Oakfield, Wisconsin
Marriage:	Sept. 2, 1836
	Eunice Goodell (d. 12/9/1837)
Children:	None
Marriage:	April 15, 1840
	Lydia Marshal
Children:	Five
Occupation:	Minister & Farmer
Dorm Room:	3 East College

Samuel Dana Darling was born February 7, 1807 in
Sterling, Massachusetts, the town in central
Massachusetts that would become famous in the 1830s
as the town that was the true basis behind the poem
"Mary Had a Little Lamb".

Samuel was the oldest of the ten children of Darius and
Susannah Darling. Although little is known of his early
life, there is little doubt that he helped shepherd his
parents' growing family as the eldest son. He and his
two brothers, Emery and Henry, no doubt were the
main labor on the family farm that included six younger
sisters and one younger brother. The youngest child,
Martha, arrived in December of 1826 when Samuel was
nearly twenty.

In 1832, at the age of twenty-five, he decided to make a
life for himself and leave the farm and family to enter
Williams College with the class of 1836. While at

Williams he was known by others as "an earnest Christian man and decided in his principles."[12] He was a man of intense and emotional temperament, while "eminently social in his nature and warm in his friendships". He was also a man of vigorous health and at times "performed some remarkable feats of strength."

A month after graduating from Williams, he met and then married Miss Eunice Goodell of West Boylston, Massachusetts on September 2, 1836. The marriage, however, was short-lived. Just barely three months after celebrating their first anniversary, Eunice passed away on December 9, 1837.

Heartbroken, Samuel moved on and studied theology at Gilmanton Theological Seminary in Gilmanton, New Hampshire, a short-lived seminary that educated students from 1835 to 1846. While in New Hampshire, he met and fell in love with Lydia Marshall of Nashua. They were married on April 20, 1840. Their marriage would produce five children, Adeline, Edward, Ellen, Samuel and George, between 1840 and 1850.

Darling was ordained as a minister early in 1841, and he moved to Cummington, Massachusetts where he settled as pastor of the First Congregational Church. On more than one occasion, he invited Mark Hopkins, President of Williams College to his church as a guest preacher.

In the spring of 1850, he felt the calling to be a missionary and moved his family to Wisconsin, continuing his work in the ministry. There he served at

---

[12] From the Williams College Biographical Annals

churches in Byron and Oakfield for the next seven years before moving once again and serving as minister of the Congregational Church in Brookfield. He served in Brookfield for three years before moving to a farm he had purchased in Oakfield, and resuming his preaching there.

In 1862, after most of the congregation of the church had entered into service for the Union army, the public services of the church were suspended, marking the close of Darling's regular work in the ministry. This was of severe regret to him.
The next year he was dealt a further blow as his son Edward, fighting for the Union with the Wisconsin regiment in the Civil War, was killed on September 20, 1863 at the battle of Chickamauga.

As Samuel Darling's health began to slowly deteriorate, he turned his affection to farming, though still preaching on occasion and giving generously to charitable causes. On May 5, 1873, he was visiting friends in Fond-du-Lac, Wisconsin. While attending a public assembly, he suddenly and unexpectedly fell to the ground, dying instantly of a rupture of the heart at the age of sixty-six.

His body was transported back to Oakfield, where he was buried in the Avoca Cemetery. He was survived by his wife, daughter Ellen, and his two sons.

Anson Loomis Hobart
Williams 1836

DR. ANSON LOOMIS HOBART '36
"The First President"

Born:	November 12, 1814
Died:	December 31, 1890 (Age 76)
Buried:	Mount Auburn Cemetery
	Cambridge, Massachusetts
Marriage:	May 10, 1838
	Ellen Brown (d. 1847)
Children:	None
Marriage:	1850
	Cordelia Perkins (d. 7/21/1878)
Children:	Four
Occupation:	Physician, Surgeon
Dorm Room:	29 East College

Anson Loomis Hobart has the distinction of being the first President of Delta Upsilon, having been elected to serve as President of the new Social Fraternity at the first meeting on November 4, 1834. He was George Clisby's roommate and brought young George along with him. After graduating with the class of 1836, he immediately became absorbed in the rigors of the outside world. First, he began teaching in academia while at the same time studying medicine, eventually leading him to medical school. He was always very absorbed in his work and for many years did not take the time to correspond with college friends, or even his Social Fraternity brothers. His page in the "Class-Record" book that lists only his name, without entry, evidences this fact. However, he always maintained an affinity for the Fraternity. In 1884, on the occasion of the Fraternity's Fiftieth Anniversary, he more than made up for lost time by sending a long and interesting letter to the Fraternity. The words of that letter are included here as a biography in Anson Hobart's own words of 1884:

"My place of birth was Columbia, New Hampshire, in 1814. I was the son of Abel and Betsy (Wallace) Hobart. My mother was Scotch and my father English, both people of blessed memory, devout Christians. I was the youngest of five sons. In youth I had the advantage of a country school. I began fitting for college in Lancaster, New Hampshire, and after a year there completed my course at Meriden. My finances were short and I eked them out by farm work. I entered Williams College with the class in 1832 and graduated with it in 1836. My fitting for college I did not enjoy very well, but I did enjoy my college course immensely. I spent all the long vacations in teaching; two winters in Sudbury, and two in Framingham, Massachusetts, and the balance of the last year in Providence, Rhode Island. After graduating I went to Freehold, New Jersey, and taught an academy five years, devoting all the time I could spare to the study of medicine, expecting to make that my profession for life. From Freehold I went to Castleton Medical College,[13] Vermont, and after two courses of lectures graduated in 1843. My medical studies I enjoyed very much, taking a deep interest in them, and finding that their difficult problems and intricacies usually gave way to earnest search and study."

During this time in medical school, his classmates recalled, with awe and envy, that Anson was always ready with difficult yet correct responses to the intricate

---

[13] Castleton Medical College was founded in 1818 and existed until 1862. It was the first medical school in Vermont and was part of what is now the current Castleton State College in Castleton, Vermont.

questions posed by the professors. This baffled classmates until they soon discovered that it was Anson's thorough study and "intense application" which gave him the mastery of the difficult subjects. Anson earned the respect and even friendship of his instructors, which he held with great value.

As he continued his letter, Hobart wrote,

"Dr. Alfred C. Post, of the New York Marine Hospital, was lecturer in the College, and when I graduated he invited me to become his assistant in the Hospital. I accepted his invitation, went with him to New York, and spent some six months in hospital practice to my great profit and delight. About this time Dr. Burnett, the only physician in Southboro, Massachusetts, died, and at a town meeting the citizens chose a committee to make inquiry and invite a physician of their choice to settle among them. From them I had a unanimous and pressing invitation to become their physician. I accepted, and at once entered into a fine practice in Southboro and all the adjoining towns. I have loved my profession so well that I wished no other preferment or office of any kind. Even the fatigues and trials, as also the triumphs, of the profession I love. In medicine I am a liberal, an independent. I take all classes of journals, and extract and cull every valuable thing from them all. And my success has been most gratifying to me. I practiced in Southboro from 1844 to 1858, fourteen years; and in Worcester, to which place I removed, from 1858 to the present, 28 years, and here I expect to remain and do so as long as I live.

I have been twice married; first to Ellen, daughter of Col. James Brown of Framingham, MA. She died suddenly

*in 1847, and went to a better world, mourned by all who
knew her. She had no children. In 1850 I married
Cordelia S. Perkins of Boston, also a lovely woman, who
became the mother of my four children, only two of whom
are now living – daughters, who remain with, and are an
unfailing comfort to me. Their mother died in 1878.
Since then I am wedded only to my profession, and a
gracious God has been my comforter."*

His good friend, Dr. James W. Brown, *Williams '40*, who
joined the Fraternity because of the influence of Anson
Hobart, would carry on a fifty-six year friendship with
him. Dr. Brown described Hobart's professional
character with these words:

*"His success as a physician and surgeon can scarcely be
paralleled. I never saw a scalpel carried by a firmer or
more skillful hand than by him, or with better
understanding of the work to be done. In his best days,
his muscular and nervous powers were almost
Herculean. He was also rich in the best of common sense
and in original inventive genius. He was largely called
in (medical) consultation and his advice was usually
implicitly followed."*

After moving to Worcester, the already respected
physician built a very large medical practice. He often
performed services for patients without expecting
anything in return. Many times the poor were sent to
his office for treatment, knowing that they could not pay
a bill, but Hobart never turned them away. He
prepared and dispensed his own medication rather than
dealing with prescriptions. His method created his own
extra work but added to the patient convenience of not

having to go to an apothecary. The needs of the patient were always first and foremost in his mind.

After the death of his wife Cordelia in 1878, Hobart remained in the company of his two daughters and focused solely on his profession, which was his only other true passion. While he had taken an active and zealous part in the early formation of the Fraternity, several years had passed since he had taken an active interest. By the middle of the 1880s, while continuing to practice, he rekindled his interest in Delta Upsilon and his classmates, even attending the fiftieth year reunion of his Williams class in 1886. He took great satisfaction in the Delta Upsilon alumni clubs of New York and Springfield, Massachusetts as well as the progress of the DU chapters at Harvard, Rutgers and Williams, even donating one thousand dollars toward the new chapter house at Williams. In 1887, at the request of the chapter, Hobart had a picture of himself commissioned by an artist and donated it to the chapter, which was hung in a place of honor in the chapter house for some time.[14] Even as late as 1888, just two years before his death, he would travel to Williamstown regularly, just to attend chapter meetings.

Little by little, he became "semi-retired" but continued to practice medicine through 1890. He began to slow down following his seventy-sixth birthday in November of 1890. After celebrating Christmas with his daughters, Mary and Cordelia, his once vigorous health began to decline rapidly. One week later on New Years Eve at his home at 42 Green Street in Worcester, Delta Upsilon's first president quietly passed away in the

---

[14] Picture shown six pages ahead. Note the DU Badge on Hobart's vest.

arms of his daughters, bringing an end to a remarkable forty-seven year career of service to others. He was laid to rest in his wife's family's plot at the historic Mount Auburn Cemetery in Cambridge.

A. L. Hobart.

REV. EPHRAIM WILLIAM KELLOGG '36
"The Recruiter"

Born:	May 2, 1811
Died:	October 10, 1887 (Age 76)
Buried:	Hillcrest Cemetery
	Heuvelton, New York
Marriage:	May, 1841
	Lois Bennett
Children:	Four
Occupation:	Minister
Dorm Room:	31 East College

Ephraim W. Kellogg was born on May 2, 1811 in
Sheffield, Massachusetts, the site of the bloodiest battle
during Shay's Rebellion in 1787. He learned to read
early in life and became a voracious reader. He was
educated at the common schools in Sheffield before
moving on to the Lenox Academy, studying there at the
same time as his future Fraternity brother, Algernon
Baldwin.

When he was eighteen years old, he began teaching at a
common school in Egremont. A year later, in 1830, he
experienced the great revivals of religion occurring in
New England churches. He was converted and joined
the Congregational Church in Sheffield. His father, Col.
Ephraim Kellogg, was very active as a deacon in that
church, and encouraged him to look to the ministry as
his life work, while promising to aid him in getting the
necessary education. As Kellogg wrote in a letter to the
Fraternity some years later, *"and so I thought that God
by his word and spirit and providence made it plain that
it was my duty to preach the gospel."*

He immediately began to prepare for college at the Egremont Academy under Ebenezer and Edward Canning and John Richards, all of them graduates of Williams College. After two years under their tutelage, in 1833, he entered Williams as a sophomore. In a later letter, he recalled fondly his time in college: *"I look back to our college course with much satisfaction. On the whole I do not think there is a much better college in the country than old Williams."* A leader in the Society, in 1835 he was elected to succeed Anson Hobart and serve as the Fraternity's second president. He would essentially recruit his roommate, Philo Canfield, as the first member to join the Fraternity after its Founding, arguably making Kellogg the first "Recruitment Chairman". He was also active in the Philologian Society, serving as President. Canfield would later join fellow Fraternity brothers Bell, Phillips and Wright at the Hartford Seminary and fulfill a career in the ministry as well.

Following his graduation in 1836, Kellogg studied theology at Auburn Theological Seminary in Auburn, New York and was licensed to preach by the Berkshire Association. He began to preach in 1840 at a Presbyterian church in Meadville, Pennsylvania. He had a call to settle there but declined it and instead returned to western New York. In May of 1841, he married Miss Lois Bennett of Auburn, New York. Together, they had two sons and two daughters, though sadly one of the sons died early in life at the age of five.

He preached in western New York for several years, where he was ordained as a pastor by the Presbytery in Buffalo on February 18, 1845. He became somewhat of an itinerant preacher, spending three to five years at a time in churches in Churchville, Millville, Lockport, Tonawanda, Oakland, Truxton, Howard and in the years after 1881 in Huevelton. He moved often, not because he was attracted to change, but because he was serving a need in the smaller churches in the region. His peers mentioned, "he preached with great earnestness and labored with great fidelity."[15]

In 1883, he suffered a minor stroke. He continued very comfortably but feebly until the end of his life. He never again took an active charge of a parish, but still preached on some occasions, even as late as the summer of 1887.

On Sunday, October 9, 1887, the good Reverend attended church like any other Sunday. Although somewhat feeble, he still enjoyed general good health. After a relaxing and uneventful day, he retired to bed as usual to rest for the next day, which he would never see. On Monday morning, October 10, 1887, his youngest daughter, Clara, who had remained unmarried and lived at home to care for her elderly parents, woke up and found her father dead in bed with his hands folded across his chest. He had passed away peacefully during the night.

Tragically though, the loss of her father greatly affected Clara. The shock of his death no doubt helped contribute to Clara's own death of heart disease one week after his. She was buried beside her father in Hillcrest Cemetery in Heuvelton, New York.

---

[15] From the <u>Williams College Obituary Record</u>

REV. JOSIAH LYMAN '36
"The Inventor"

Born: October 9, 1811
Died: October 6, 1889 (Age 78)
Buried: Main Street Cemetery
                    Easthampton, Massachusetts
Marriage: May 22, 1844
                    Mary Bingham
Children: Two
Occupation: Teacher, Minister, Engineer and
                    Businessman
Dorm Room: 25 East College

Josiah Lyman was arguably one of the more "natural geniuses" of all of the Founding Fathers. He had to be, as the standards of the Lyman family were always set very high. He was also the first member of the Fraternity to establish a fraternal "legacy", as his brothers Addison Lyman, *Williams 1839*, and Horace Lyman, *Williams 1842*, followed him as members of the Social Fraternity. Fellow Founder, Lyndon Lyman, was of no relation.

He was born in the family farm house at 45 Park Hill Road in Easthampton, Massachusetts on October 9, 1811, the son of Daniel and Sally (Clapp) Lyman. Both parents were six generations removed from their ancestors who arrived on the *Mayflower*; "all of whom were in direct line of the true Pilgrim spirit as well as lineage."[16] With a good strong family background, Lyman was also well grounded and had the benefit of a good education.

---

[16] From the <u>Williams College Biographical Annals</u>

Josiah Lyman
Williams 1836

*Image courtesy of Williams College
Archives and Special Collections*

He attended the common schools in Easthampton, some of which had secondary grade levels, which was not always common in most towns. After his public schooling, he prepared for college at Southampton, Massachusetts where he spent two years primarily studying Greek and Latin alongside future Fraternity brother, Lebbeus Phillips, *Williams 1836.*

After his studies at Southampton, he entered Williams College in 1832 a very focused and diligent student. He possessed a natural ability for math and mechanical engineering, and was especially drawn to geometry and astronomy. Even with his natural intellect and devotion to learning, he was extremely devout in his religious practices and was "a Christian of unblemished character." It was said that everyone who knew him professed full confidence in his abilities. He and Edmund Wright, *Williams 1836,* his Williams College roommate and childhood friend from Easthampton, would both join the Social Fraternity's effort together in November of 1834.

After graduating in 1836, he spent two years teaching in Canaan, New York. In the fall of 1839, he returned to Easthampton where he opened and successfully ran an English and Classical Studies school of his own. This venture was short-lived, however, as he began to feel a calling to the ministry.

Deciding on a life as a minister, he enrolled at the Auburn Theological Seminary in New York in October of 1842 and stayed there for two years after he was licensed to preach. During his time at the seminary, he also took charge of and taught at an academy in Bristol, Connecticut. He relished the opportunity to share the

Gospel with students, converting nearly thirty of them during his three terms there. This ability to influence the "spiritual good" of his students and others he came in contact with, led him to finally choose teaching as a permanent profession, while still reserving the right to preach on occasion as an ordained minister.

In 1844, he took over as Principal of an academy in Williston, Vermont, where he stayed for three years. While there, he met Mary Bingham of Cornwall, Vermont. After a short courtship, Josiah and Mary were married on May 22, 1844. On Christmas Eve a year later, their son, Albert, was born, while their daughter, Sarah, followed in January of 1848. Josiah and Mary's shared faith made a profound impact on their children's spiritual life as well. Albert would grow to become the pastor of the South Congregational Church in Brooklyn, New York, while Sarah would marry a minister in Massachusetts.

In 1847, Josiah moved again, and for two years he took charge of the Lenox Academy where his Fraternity Brothers Baldwin and Kellogg had once studied. During this time, his love of teaching was hindered by ill health due to overwork, which forced him to step aside and find something to do that would be a little less taxing. So, in 1849, he took up the "hobby" of civil engineering.

Because of his burning interest in astronomy, he began to look at the idea of manufacturing refracting telescopes. By 1850 he had finished building a sixteen-foot sample, at that time determined to be the finest and largest ever made in the United States. It soon became the model for refracting telescopes. Continuing with his newfound "hobby", he soon invented and developed the Protracting Trigonometer. Through his continued perfecting and development over the next eight or nine years, his patented invention became the best drafting instrument up to that time in the U.S. and Europe in terms of convenience and accuracy. Ironically, as a young college student, he envisioned a life long career in teaching or the ministry, yet he ended up spending nearly forty years – half of his life – in the development and manufacture of scientific instruments like trigonometers, protracting telescopes and Herschelian telescopes. In 1862, he also published A Manual of the Protracting Trigonometer, that included a written recommendation from his Delta Upsilon fraternity brother Zalmon Richards, *Williams 1836* within its seventy-seven pages.

By 1886, he had moved back to the family farm on Park Hill in Easthampton, where his brother Lauren lived. Josiah contracted pneumonia and died on October 6, 1889, in the home where he was born, just three days shy of his birthday. He was survived by his wife and two children. An impressive monument marks his grave in the family plot in Main Street Cemetery in Easthampton, Massachusetts.

Lyman Family Home – Easthampton, Massachusetts

Josiah Lyman,

REV. LEBBEUS RUDE PHILLIPS '36
"The Eldest Brother"

Born:	November 1, 1806
Died:	September 7, 1886 (Age 79)
Buried:	Cremated
Marriage:	July 24, 1838
	Susannah Goddard (d. 8/25/1901)
Children:	Four
Occupation:	Minister
Dorm Room:	19 East College

A native of Ashfield, Massachusetts, Lebbeus Rude Phillips, named after his maternal grandfather, Lebbeus Rude, was born on November 1, 1806, the second of the ten children of Elijah and Fanny Rude Phillips. He spent his childhood in what he called "an obscure town among the hills of Western Massachusetts". At the age of nine or ten, after sitting in a church and hearing an eloquent preacher, he made a decision at that moment to become a minister himself one day. Although he admitted from that point forward that his *"star of hope shone pretty dimly,"* he remained resolute that he was to be a minister.

However, being the second-born and the eldest son, his father depended on him for help with family obligations and work around the home. As a result, his opportunities for schooling in his early years were both meager and sporadic. By the time the other children in his family were old enough to shoulder family burdens, Lebbeus had reached the age of twenty-three.

Lebbeus Rude Phillips
Williams 1836

*Image courtesy of Williams College
Archives and Special Collections*

It was at this time that he began to study at Ashfield Academy, while also holding down a job to earn money for his educational expenses. His studies at Ashfield were followed by further study at schools in New Ipswich, New Hampshire and Southampton, Massachusetts, where he would meet future Fraternity Brother, Josiah Lyman. In 1832, he and Lyman both enrolled at Williams College.

At Williams, Phillips had the high esteem of his fellow classmates and others at the college, and was known for being a good student. He was said to have had a "fine voice, and was noted for his excellence in elocution." During his sophomore year, he received the Moonlight Prize[17] for speaking, which he noted as being his "only college honor". After graduating from Williams, along with fellow Fraternity brother Hiram Bell and others, he entered the East Windsor Theological Institute[18] in Connecticut.

In 1838, while in his second year of seminary, he married Susannah Goddard of Roxbury, Massachusetts. Their marriage produced four children, two sons and two daughters. Their son, Edward, arrived in 1840, followed by daughter, Catherine, in 1842. After Edward's death at the age of three in 1843, the Phillips' welcomed fraternal twins with daughter, Helen, and son, John, in 1848. John would later go on to graduate

---

[17] Juniors and sophomores competed in an oratorical contest the day before commencement. The winner of the contest was announced the next day. The name "Moonlight Prize" came from the fact that the contest was held in the evening after dark.

[18] Now Hartford Seminary in Hartford, Connecticut

from Williams like his father,[19] and would become a highly successful shipping merchant.

After graduating from the seminary, Phillips preached in Halifax, Vermont, where he was called and ordained on July 25, 1841. He became the pastor of the Congregational Church in Sharon, Massachusetts, where he ministered for twenty years. Then, in about 1861, his impaired and declining health forced him to step down as full time minister in Sharon. He moved to Groton, Massachusetts where he lived for nearly another sixteen years and preached on occasion in Auburndale and Newtonville as his health permitted. He retired fully from the pulpit in 1877.

For the last few years of his life, this excellent speaker suffered from what was probably meningitis, gradually causing both mental and physical suffering in his final two years. In 1886, he traveled to Amherst, Massachusetts to visit and spend the summer with his brother, Augustine. In the middle of August, the meningitis transitioned into paralysis. Reverend Phillips lingered for about three weeks before succumbing to the disease on September 6, 1886; two months shy of his eightieth birthday. He was survived by his beloved wife of forty-eight years, daughter Catherine and son John. Twin daughter Helen had died in 1881.

His body was transported back to Groton, and in a practice that was relatively new and uncommon for the time period, is believed to have been cremated with his

---

[19] John would not follow in his father's footsteps as a member of DU, since the Williams Chapter was dormant from 1862 to 1883.

ashes being scattered on his property in Groton. His wife Susannah would join her husband in the same manner fifteen years later in 1901.

Zalmon Richards
Williams 1836

Image courtesy of Williams College
Archives and Special Collections

ZALMON RICHARDS '36
"The Educator"

Born:	August 11, 1811
Died:	November 1, 1899 (Age 88)
Buried:	Oak Hill Cemetery
	Washington, D.C.
Marriage:	November 14, 1836
	Minerva A. Todd (d. 1873)
Children:	None
Marriage:	August 19, 1874
	Mary F. Mather (d. 8/4/1898)
Children:	George M.
Occupation:	Educator, Administrator
Dorm Room:	18 East College

One of only two of the ten Founders of the Class of 1836 to not pursue a life in the ministry, Zalmon Richards was certainly the most public figure of his fraternal class. He was the only one of Delta Upsilon's Founders, to have founded not one, but <u>two</u> national organizations.

He was born in Cummington, Massachusetts on August 11, 1811, the son of Nehemiah and Betsey (Packard) Richards. Through both parents he was a descendent of a long line of deacons and ministers, who had an impact not on his career, but certainly on his life.

He was known to throw his whole effort into things he believed in. When the beginnings of the Social Fraternity were taking place, he no doubt was the one who zealously influenced his roommate David

91

Pise to join the effort, rather than the other way around.

Like some of the other Founders of the Fraternity that lived well past the Fiftieth Anniversary of the Founding, we are fortunate to have an account of his life, in his own words:

"My early life was on a farm and in a tannery. At the age of sixteen I was put to learning the trade of brick-laying and plastering. Perhaps the world would have been just as well off had I continued in that employment. I know, however, that I have felt the influence and the benefit of that trade ever since. During one of the winters of my apprenticeship I attended the Cummington Academy, then in charge of the Rev. Rosewell Hawkes, a graduate of Williams College, who had the indiscretion, or may I say, the foresight into my future, to urge me to go through a course of college training. This was an idea, and an inspiration, which I could not shake off; nor did I try much to do so, though I was aware that my father's large family and limited means, would not permit him to help me much in the necessary expenses.

At the age of eighteen, however, I formed the purpose, in which afterwards I never faltered, that I would, trusting in God, enter upon a college course on my own responsibility. I was encouraged in this by the fact that I had been successful, as a New England teacher, from my seventeenth year, though regarding myself as but poorly qualified. When I was twenty my father gave me my time, so that I might take such course as I chose, but without promising any pecuniary aid. I launched my vessel, however, alone upon the treacherous sea of life,

*always keeping a good lookout for breakers, with heart
and will for any fate.*

*I fitted for college, poorly indeed, in one year, and
entered with the class in October 1832. In my first two
years I had some pecuniary aid, in the form of a loan;
but before the end of my college course I was enabled to
discharge this, and to meet my current expenses, by the
avails of my teaching and manual labor. I believed that
I could help myself. I know that my purposes were good,
and strove to act accordingly, and to hold myself ready
for any work to which God might call me.*

*My recollections of college life are all pleasant. I never
can forget the noble men in the College faculty. I ought
not to particularize, but I must acknowledge my great
indebtedness to Dr. Mark Hopkins and the many kind
words of our noble and venerable President, Dr. Griffin,
who often sent for me to trim the graceful, snowy locks
upon his great head. It is not alone the Greek or Latin,
or words of our text-books which I remember with so
much satisfaction at the home of our dear Alma Mater,
but the lessons of mind, of heart, of high Christian
character, which were so well exemplified in our
instructors."*

Just before graduating from Williams College, Richards
purchased all of the shares of the Academy in
Cummington, Massachusetts where he grew up, and
upon graduation from Williams, he set himself up in his
chosen career as an educator. This venture, however,
was just the beginning. It was at Cummington
Academy where he employed as his assistant, Miss
Minerva A. Todd, who had just graduated with honors
from the Charlestown Female Seminary in

Massachusetts. A few months after her hiring, he and Minerva married, and continued to work together at the Academy. They built up not only a successful school and fine reputations, but were also very successful financially with the Academy.

In 1838, Richards and his wife moved and took over the Stillwater Academy in New York, where they served hundreds of bright students for ten years, again enjoying incredible success. Under their direction the institution flourished, and Richards caught the attention of several Regents from the University of New York, as well as the Governor of Vermont. While at Stillwater, he was called to be Superintendent of the first ever Teachers Institute in the county. There Richards would later recall, *"...I think I did some of the most valuable work of my life."*

In 1849, he left Stillwater and assumed the leadership of the Preparatory Department of Columbia College in Washington, D.C., and his wife opened a school for young ladies, called the "Union Female Academy." After his work at Columbia College,[20] Zalmon began the Union School for Young Men in 1855. It was of this venture that he wrote, *"We think we had our most marked success, professionally and financially."* However, his next effort is likely the one for which he could easily be the most heralded.

In 1857, Richards joined forces with several other committed educators to form the National Education Association (NEA), and Richards was elected as its first President. Today, the NEA is one of the largest

---

[20] Now a part of George Washington University

educational associations in the world. Former President of Stanford University and Delta Upsilon brother David Starr Jordan, *Cornell 1872*, would also later serve as NEA President from 1914 to 1915. In addition, Richards also apparently had a hand in the early development of the Young Men's Christian Association (YMCA) in the United States, serving as the first President of a local chapter.

Zalmon Richards was elected to the Common Council of the city of Washington, D.C and was made its President in 1860. A year later, as the Civil War broke out, Richards became connected with the U.S. Treasury Department, under United States Treasury Secretary, Salmon P. Chase. There he served as a clerk for about six years before leaving to accept a job serving directly under Dr. Henry Barnard, who had been appointed as the first United States Commissioner of Education. While a clerk for Commissioner Barnard, Richards was elected to the Board of Aldermen for the District of Columbia and helped to create the "Office of Public Schools" (School District). He was subsequently appointed by the Mayor to serve as the first school Superintendent from 1869 to 1870. In addition, he also served a three-year stint as Auditor for the District of Columbia.

Early in 1873, after thirty-six years of marriage and great career success with his wife, Minerva fell ill and died. Within that same year, several others in his family also passed away. His emotional loss was considerable, and his personal wealth beginning to dwindle, as he had become the guardian for a young lady, supposedly a relative, who had become insolvent. In addition, he lost a considerable amount of his large property holdings due to his overconfidence in supporting a business friend. Nevertheless, through courage and faith, he remained focused and positive.

In August 1874 he married Mary F. Mather, of Darien, Connecticut and a descendant of the famous New England puritan minister, Cotton Mather. Richards and his new wife, twenty-four years his junior, began the Eclectic Seminary with their collective passion for education. Regarding these difficult times, he wrote: *"I have never lost my confidence in God. My health of body, mind, and soul has never been better than now, we have a comfortable, unencumbered home in this beautiful city, and the other untold comforts, and are now pleasantly engaged in teaching children and youth in our own "Eclectic Seminary." I think I never knew better than now how to teach."* Together he and Mary maintained a home at 1401 New York Avenue in Washington D.C. and had a son, George, when Zalmon was nearly seventy years old and Mary forty-four.

Richards had accomplished more than the normal man in his lifetime. In addition to his already numerous accomplishments, he had written for many educational journals and had published a "Manual for Elementary Schools" as well as an arithmetic textbook. He remained dedicated to the cause of education throughout his entire life.

In August of 1898, a week before Zalmon's eighty-eighth birthday, Mary passed away and was buried alongside her parents in the Mather Cemetery in Darien, Connecticut. Zalmon continued on, and a year later celebrated his eighty-ninth birthday in August with his son. Two and a half months later on November 1, at

4:15 am, Zalmon Richards quietly passed away at his home, bringing to a close one of the more storied lives of an educational leader.

After a funeral at the E Street Baptist Church, he was quietly laid to rest in the historic Oak View Cemetery in Washington, D.C., about ten feet from the grave of Edwin M. Stanton; President Abraham Lincoln's noted Secretary of War who upon the death of Lincoln uttered the famous words, "Now he belongs to the ages." The same could be said of Richards.

Adding yet another first to this esteemed Delta Upsilon Founder's accolades, Zalmon would also be the first to produce an offspring that would follow his fraternal legacy when his beloved son George joined Delta Upsilon at Williams College, graduating with the class of 1904.

The house at 1301 Corcoran Street NW in Washington, D.C. where the Richards family moved in 1890, still stands today. It was designated as a National Historic Landmark in 1965. The "Zalmon Richards House" is a fitting tribute to the first president of the NEA and one of the premier educators of his time.

The plaque on the Zalmon Richards House in
Washington, D.C., declaring it a National
Historic Landmark

The Zalmon Richards House at 1301 Corcoran
Street NW in Washington , D.C.

REV. EDMUND WRIGHT '36
"The Missionary"

Born:	July 1, 1808
Died:	July 20, 1901 (Age 93)
Buried:	Lake View Cemetery
	Seattle, Washington
Marriage:	August 1842
	Achsah F. Hurd
Children:	Four
Occupation:	Minister
Dorm Room:	25 East College

Like seven other Founders of the Class of 1836, Edmund
Wright was also destined to become a minister. He was
the third of five sons and was born in Easthampton,
Massachusetts on July 1, 1808. Both of his parents,
Ichabod and Mary, were "devout and earnest
Christians." Perhaps his character is best described by
the following passage from a Williams College
biographical sketch:

*"Edmund was a son worthy of such parents. His early
religious history, if written out in detail, would be one of
very great interest, bringing to view his long and severe
struggle under conviction of sin, his decision at last for
Christ and his service, his coming into the light and
peace and hope of the gospel, and his entrance at once
upon Christian work among his schoolfellows and
others, doing the work of an evangelist, and that with a
wonderful success even before he had reached his
majority. Certainly no sketch of him, while in college,
would be complete or be recognized by his old associates,
which did not bring into prominence his uniform,*

Edmund Wright
Williams 1836

*Image courtesy of Williams College
Archives and Special Collections*

earnest, and consistent piety, piety not obtrusive or morose, but manly, genial, making his face to shine, and gaining for him the confidence and esteem of his fellow students. It was a matter of course that he should have the ministry in view as his life-work."

In his early years, he was fortunate to have the opportunity to attend common school. He subsequently prepared for college at Hopkins Academy in Hadley, Massachusetts, followed by schooling at the Amherst Academy, where he completed his college preparation. During this time, he taught in the winter months to meet his expenses. He was said to be a very diligent and faithful student, and "stood well as a scholar among his classmates."[21]

He enrolled in Williams in 1832 and joined the Fraternity, likely as a joint effort with his roommate and childhood friend from Easthampton, Josiah Lyman. Wright was the second brother to establish a fraternal legacy, as his younger brother would follow him not only to Williams, but into the Social Fraternity as well. Russell Wright, *Williams 1841,* would later serve both as vice-president and president of the Williams Chapter.

Edmund's life after graduation from Williams is probably best described in his own words in a letter to a friend and classmate, where he sketched his life and career:

---

[21] From the <u>Williams College Obituary Record</u>

"I studied Theology at the Theological Institute, at East Windsor Connecticut.[22] Having graduated there I left New England for Missouri in 1839, and labored as a City Missionary in St. Louis until April of 1841. During several months following I visited some forty counties in the state organizing Sabbath Schools, and for a few months ministered to the Presbyterian Church in Palmyra, Missouri. In October of 1842 I entered upon the work of a missionary and pastor in Weston, Platte County, near Fort Leavenworth, where I remained until November of 1849, about seven years.

I then returned to St. Louis and became Pastor of the Spruce Street Presbyterian Church, remaining until May of 1856. A month later I began to labor as agent of the American Tract Society, and continued in that service over two and a half years. Owing to ill health I then sought rest, assuming no public labor until May 1863, when I became agent of the American Bible Society for Missouri..."

In August of 1842, Miss Achsah F. Hurd of Bridgeport, Vermont became Mrs. Edmund Wright. They had three daughters, Mary, Emma and Anna and one son. Their only son Edmund, a promising young physician who was attending Williams College, was forced to leave college during his freshman year due to failing health, and died awhile later in 1876.

Edmund Wright stayed with the American Bible Society for a few more years, retiring in about 1890. By 1892, the Wrights had moved from St. Louis to Sidney,

---

[22] Now the Hartford Seminary in Hartford, Connecticut, where Wright attended with his Fraternity Brothers, Hiram Bell and Lebbeus Phillips.

Nebraska, a place they would call home for only a few years. Their final move took them to a house at 514 Light Street (now 2nd Avenue) in Seattle, Washington to live with Wright's only living daughter, Anna Whitney, and her husband and two sons. Wright maintained his great interest in the Fraternity, even writing to the *Delta Upsilon Quarterly* in 1894, when he reported: *"of the ten D.U. members in Williams '36, Zalmon Richards, of Washington, D.C., and myself are the only survivors."*

After Richards' death in 1899, Edmund Wright became the sole survivor of the class of 1836 and the oldest remaining of the original thirty. On January 1, 1901, he would also become one of only four Founders to see the twentieth century.

Edmund Wright passed away quietly on July 20 at the age of ninety-three and was buried in Lake View Cemetery in Seattle. Survived by his wife and daughter, Edmund Wright lived longer than any of the Founders. Upon his death, he was eulogized with this remembrance of his character: "Kindness, gentleness, cheerfulness of disposition, temperate in his every act, and a true Christian made him a model husband and a loving father. He is mourned by thousands who learned to know him by his Christian kindness and love him for himself alone."[23]

---

[23] From the <u>Williams College Obituary Record</u>

The Class of 1837

Daniel Brown

Solomon Clark

Edward Clarke

Stephen Johnson Field

Lewis Conger Lockwood

Lyndon Graves Lyman

Henry Morgan

William Henry Noble

Comfort Sparks

Francis Wilder Tappan

The Sophomores

The class of 1837, or "the second ten of one of the three lower classes" at Williams in November of 1834, are by far the most intriguing and tragic group of the three. Their sheer diversity, both in their chosen professions and their individual characters, makes them stand out as the most exciting.

For starters, this sophomore class had only a seventy percent graduation rate, the lowest of the three. Also lower was the percentage of ministers that were produced from this class. Only fifty percent or exactly half of the sophomores pursued a theological path, compared to eighty percent for each of the other two classes.

The remaining five who did not pursue a religious career path include a dentist, an engineer and three lawyers, all of whom would rise to a position on a judicial bench. Four of this class died before the age of 62 while the remaining six each lived into their eighties.

At Williams, these ten were the energy behind the idea of forming the Fraternity, providing the steam to move forward.

In this class, one would find the authors of the first Social Fraternity Constitution, the host of the first organizational meeting and the catalyst who essentially started and was the brainchild behind this "non-secret idea".

These men were the "most care free" of them all, as care free as one could be in that time period. One could argue that "care free" also meant "fearless". They were the hull of the ship that provided the strength and stability to carry the load. They were the ones who provided the vision and the connection to the other two classes. At the same time, they were the ones who provided the energy and wherewithal to get things started. Without the members of the sophomore class, Delta Upsilon would never have been founded in the first place.

They were the driving force...

REV. DANIEL BROWN '37
"Co-Author of the Constitution"

Born: July 23, 1813
Died: November 8, 1846 (Age 33)
Buried: Hillside Cemetery
                  Cortlandt Manor, New York
Marriage: April 15, 1839
                  Susan Tompkins
Children: One
Occupation: Minister
Dorm Room: 11 West College

Daniel Brown hailed from the tiny village of Nelson, New Hampshire where he was born on July 23, 1813. He grew up in New Hampshire and lived there until the age of twenty, when he moved away from his family to enroll at Williams in the fall of 1833. While at Williams he felt the call to become a minister, as was common of the typical Williams student at that time.

Sharing room number eleven in West College with his roommate Lyndon Lyman, Brown was part of a "package deal" in joining the Social Fraternity in November of 1834. He would take an active part in the Fraternity and would be a significant contributor to the effort, although he likely would never take credit for it. Nonetheless, shortly after the formation of the Fraternity, Daniel Brown volunteered to join forces with fellow member Edward Clarke in authoring the Fraternity's new Constitution.

The two men quickly, eloquently and methodically put the thoughts and ideals of the new group on paper, a writing that led to the roadmap that future generations would follow.[24]

He completed his studies in four years, graduating in the spring of 1837, and moved to New York to begin the next stage of his education. He took a rather atypical path and began private theological study rather than attending a seminary. He prided himself on the simplicity and humbleness by which he went about his life. Rather than attend formal seminary, for three years he studied and learned the practice of ministry under the watchful eye and guide of an ordained minister in a local parish. During this time he met and fell in love with Susan Tompkins, whom he married on April 15, 1839. Six months later, on October 23, he was ordained as a Presbyterian minister in Somers, New York.

Life seemed to be going well for the young married couple. Following his ordination, Daniel and his wife moved to Peekskill, New York where he was called to serve a small Presbyterian parish. For the next four years, he and Susan set up their home and established roots in Peekskill. Then, in March of 1843 they became the proud parents of a son, Edward Payson Brown.

The joy that they felt by the addition of this little boy to their family would not last long, however, as little Edward died suddenly on September 24, 1845 at the tender age of two and a half.

---

[24] The result of their collective efforts may be found in the appendix of this book.

The following year, on November 8, 1846, Reverend Daniel Brown passed away as well, probably of cholera, leaving his widow Susan alone to mourn the loss of the two men in her life.

Susan Brown never remarried, but instead lived as a widow for thirty-five more years. Susan passed away December 16, 1881 at the age of sixty-eight and was buried next to her husband and son at Hillside Cemetery in Cortlandt Manor, New York.

Solomon Clark
Williams 1837

REV. SOLOMON CLARK '37
"The Historian"

Born:	March 2, 1811
Died:	December 7, 1902 (Age 91)
Buried:	Hilltop Cemetery
	Plainfield, Massachusetts
Marriage:	May 5, 1841
	Elizabeth Haven
Marriage:	October 5, 1858
	Lucy Elvira Gilbert
Children:	One
Occupation:	Minister
Dorm Room:	32 West College

Little is known about the son of Luther Clark, other than that he was named after his maternal grandfather when he was born on March 2, 1811. Interestingly, his birth took place in Northampton, Massachusetts on the present site of Smith College, the alma mater of former United States First Ladies Nancy Reagan and Barbara Bush.

Solomon Clark prepared for college in Northampton before enrolling in Williams College in 1833. He and his roommate, Edward Clarke, shared much in common besides their homonymic last names. Both were from neighboring towns in Massachusetts. Both would pursue ministerial careers and serve pastorates in Congregational Churches. Both would graduate from Williams and attend the same seminary. So, it was only natural that the two of them would also join the Fraternity together, with Solomon joining at the behest of Edward, due to the latter's connection to Stephen

Field, and being one of the first to know about the idea of forming this new fraternity.

After his graduation from Williams in 1837, he and Edward Clarke joined four of their Fraternity brothers at the Hartford Theological Seminary in East Windsor, Connecticut to prepare for the ministry. Solomon was ordained April 14, 1841 and became pastor of the Congregational Church in Petersham, Massachusetts. Three weeks later, on May 5, 1841, he married his fiancée, Elizabeth Haven. Together they served the church in Petersham for ten years.

Sometime thereafter, in the early 1850s, Elizabeth passed away, leaving the widower pastor alone and childless. Seeking a new parish and a fresh start, he relocated to South Canton, Massachusetts, where he served a church for seven years. In January of 1858, he was called to a pastorate in Plainfield, Massachusetts. It was in Plainfield where he would find happiness again and serve comfortably for another eighteen years.

After arriving in Plainfield, Solomon met and befriended Mrs. Lucy Gilbert and her three children, Flora, George and Foster. Lucy had been married to W.C. Gilbert since the early 1840s. It is not known whether divorce or death separate W.C. and Lucy, but what is known, is that Solomon Clark and Lucy Gilbert fell in love. They married on October 5, 1858, and together they would have one daughter, Elizabeth, likely named in memory of Solomon's first wife.

During his time in Plainfield, he wrote "Old Testament Chronology," published in the *Boston Recorder* in 1863, and then "Memorial of Susan Woods Vining" in 1866.

His final pastorate was to a church in Goshen, Massachusetts, where he preached for six years before retiring from the ministry in 1882. In addition to being a fine pastor, he always had a great interest in history. After his retirement, he moved back to Northampton where he lived for a few years, enjoying his second passion. He wrote many historical articles that were published in the *Puritan Recorder, Boston Recorder,* and the *American Messenger,* and he even acted as the Plainfield correspondent for the *Hampshire Gazette.* In addition, he authored <u>Antiquities, Historicals and Graduates of Northampton</u>, a 380 page book published in 1882, followed in 1891 by the 239 page <u>Historical Catalogue of the Northampton First Church, 1661 – 1891</u>.

By the latter part of the 1890s, old age began to slow Solomon and his wife. They decided to move to Chicago, Illinois to live with their daughter, Elizabeth. It was here that Solomon and Lucy lived for the remainder of their years.

He remained interested in the affairs of the Fraternity, however. He was proud to be a Founder and knew that the effort had grown since he and Edward Clarke had emerged from Room Thirty-Two and made their way downstairs to the Freshman Recitation Room so many years ago. By 1902, he was one of only three of the Founders still living, all of whom hailed from the class of 1837. He, along with Brothers Lockwood and Tappan, were invited by the Fraternity to attend the seventieth convention of Delta Upsilon, held in Chicago in 1904. Since Solomon was a resident of Chicago, it seemed logical that he would attend if he survived that long. Sadly, he did not.

Solomon Clark passed away on December 7, 1902 at the age of ninety-one. His body was returned to Plainfield, Massachusetts and buried in Hilltop Cemetery in sight of the church where he had long served as its faithful pastor. Lucy would follow him into repose seven months later and be buried by his side.

This excerpt from the eulogy given at his burial service provides a good glimpse into his character: *"Both as a gentleman and citizen, and as a faithful and successful pastor I have heard the name of no other minister who preceded me spoken more frequently, and always in terms of the highest appreciation and affection. His loyalty to Christ and devotion to His work, his sympathy as a friend and fidelity in ministering to all the temporal and spiritual needs of his people, the simplicity and sincerity of his personal character, all have been made apparent in the things that have been said of him...his ministry was fruitful in winning men to Christ.*

"He had a respect for and sympathy with those who differed. He sought to persuade, rather than compel men. He gave due credit to honesty and integrity of purpose and life. He was interested in the larger life of the community, as well as in the up-building of the church."

Plainfield Congregational Church
Plainfield, Massachusetts

REV. EDWARD CLARKE '37
"The Parliamentarian"

Born:	July 10, 1810
Died:	January 11, 1891 (Age 80)
Buried:	Oak Grove Cemetery
	Springfield, Massachusetts
Marriage:	April 18, 1839
	Diantha Jenkins (d. 1843)
Marriage:	March 12, 1844
	Julia Hyde
Children:	Number unknown
Occupation:	Minister
Dorm Room:	32 West College

Edward Clarke was born July 10, 1810 in Chesterfield, Massachusetts, the son of Olive and Richard Clarke, a prosperous farmer in the area. Edward, like fellow Founder Zalmon Richards, prepared for college at Cummington Academy before enrolling at Williams College with his best friend, Stephen J. Field. Clarke and Field would remain the best of friends throughout their lifetime. Clarke was never one to sit idly by, and was a model for perseverance. This perseverance made it fitting for him to join the effort of the developing Social Fraternity, and subsequently influenced his roommate, Solomon Clark, to join as well. His leadership qualities made him the natural selection to draft the Fraternity's first Constitution with Daniel Brown, although Clarke would likely be the one to organize and champion the effort and serve as the first "parliamentarian" of sorts.

After his graduation from Williams, he went on to study theology at the Hartford Theological Seminary, where he and Solomon Clark joined fellow Founders Hiram Bell, Lebbeus Phillips and Edmund Wright. Upon leaving the seminary, he married Miss Diantha Jenkins of Cummington, Massachusetts on April 18, 1839. His marriage was followed by his ordination two months later as pastor of the Congregational Church at Middlefield, Massachusetts. There he would preach for thirteen years and oversee the construction of a new church building. His pastorate, however, would last longer than his marriage. In 1843, after just barely three years together, Diantha passed away.

Apparently not finding bachelorhood appealing, he soon married his second wife, the former Miss Julia Hyde, on March 12, 1844. The marriage produced children, none of whom survived the couple.

In 1852, he began preaching at the Congregational Church in Ashfield, where he again supervised the construction project of a new building. His pastorate lasted only two years, however, as ill health required him to take some time off. When he had regained his health, he moved again and accepted the charge of the Huntington Hill Church in Huntington, Massachusetts. He served there during the Civil War years before returning to Middlefield to again take charge of his original church and care for his elderly parents, both in their eighties. In 1870, while still preaching, he was elected to the Massachusetts State Legislature, where he served one term. In 1872, with his own health in decline, he was forced to resign his pastorate to coincide with the end of his congressional term.

For the next ten years, Edward Clarke suffered from chronic laryngitis. He continued to care for his aged parents while preaching on occasion, when his voice would allow. In 1876, his father passed away at the age of ninety.

Six years later, in 1882, Edward moved to Springfield, Massachusetts with his wife and ninety-six year old mother. There they all joined the Olivet Church, and he occasionally filled in there and at other neighborhood churches as a supply preacher when needed. He continued to care for his very spry mother until she passed away in January of 1887, at the age of one hundred and one.

Former Congressman Clarke ignored the fact of his own ill health and age of over seventy-five years. He made one last trip from Massachusetts to Washington D.C. to visit his best friend, Fraternity brother and college classmate, Stephen J. Field, who was by this time a long-serving justice on the United States Supreme Court. Despite suffering from Bright's disease,[25] Clarke continued to maintain his usual cheery and generous disposition without complaint. As the oldest congregational minister in Western Massachusetts, he kept on with the Lord's work. Just after New Year's Day in 1891, he took a trip to downtown Springfield on a streetcar. He caught a cold, which quickly manifested into influenza. Undaunted, he continued to visit friends for the next two days before becoming bedridden on January 8. Three days later, battling Bright's disease and the flu, he passed away at his home at 584 State Street in Springfield, Massachusetts. He was buried in

---

[25] A kidney disease more commonly called Nephritis in present day.

the front section of Oak Grove Cemetery, near the site of his home.

Since the Clarke Family was known for their longevity and his parents both living into their nineties, Edward Clarke passed away at the relatively young age of eighty. He was survived by his wife Julia, a one-hundred-two-year-old uncle and his nearly one-hundred-five-year-old aunt.

HON. STEPHEN JOHNSON FIELD '37
"The Founder"

Born:	November 4, 1816
Died:	April 9, 1899 (Age 82)
Buried:	Rock Creek Cemetery
	Washington, D.C.
Marriage:	June 2, 1859
	Sue Virginia Swearingen
Children:	None
Occupation:	Lawyer / Judge
Dorm Room:	23 West College

The life of Stephen Johnson Field cannot adequately be told here. Field was without a doubt the highest profiled individual of all of the Founders. He also may very well have been the most controversial. He came from one of the most prominent families of the nineteenth century and rose to a level of national prominence in his own right.

Field was the sixth of nine children of David and Submit Dickinson Field, four of whom achieved national prominence. In addition to Stephen's accomplishments, his older brother David was a U.S. Congressman and law reformer, and Brother Cyrus was a businessman and industrialist who successfully laid the first telegraph cable across the Atlantic Ocean. Youngest brother Henry was a noted author and clergyman. Stephen was born exactly eighteen years before the Founding, on November 4, 1816 in Haddam, Connecticut, where the family lived before moving to Stockbridge, Massachusetts.

Stephen Johnson Field
Williams 1837

It was only natural for Stephen Field to attend Williams College as the Field family had many ties to the College. Field's father, David, had a good friend who was a founding Trustee of the College, and their neighbors in Stockbridge were the Hopkins Family. Mark and Albert Hopkins would both grow up to teach at Williams, with Mark later serving as the longest tenured President in Williams College history at thirty-six years. The father of the College's founder, Ephraim Williams, was also a neighbor of the Fields.

Stephen's older brother David Dudley Field Jr., was the first to enroll at Williams, graduating with the class of 1824, a year behind Mark Hopkins. Younger brother Jonathan Edwards Field would graduate with the class of 1832. Stephen was already a world traveler before enrolling at Williams himself in 1833, having spent two years in Turkey with his sister Emilia, studying Greek, French and Italian.

As a family, the Field brothers had a mischievous spirit, which apparently set the tone for Stephen. While at Williams, he was put on four month probation for "blowing a horn in the halls" as well as for "injuring a building".[26] The sanctions were later dropped, however, after Field publicly apologized. Field was very bright and extremely popular in college, but was determined, stubborn and even vengeful when he was crossed. Almost immediately upon his arrival at Williams, he took an interest in the flavor and student politics of the college. This interest, in part, led to the formation of the Social Fraternity.

---

[26] Details of these two incidents are unknown.

In 1837, Stephen graduated as the valedictorian of his class and joined his older brother, David, in New York City to study law and earn his law degree. It was David who encouraged Stephen to travel west to the territory of California and offered to fund his travel expenses. Stephen accepted his brother's offer, but first set out for a year-long trip to Europe in 1848 before returning to the United States, and subsequently arriving in San Francisco.

He moved north to an area named Marysville and within three days became the town's *alcalde*,[27] the chief administrator of a town who carried on both the judicial and the administrative duties. As essentially the new mayor and judge of the town, Field had his hands full in the midst of the California gold rush in 1849. Being relatively unsettled territory where duels typically decided disputes, Stephen frequently carried two pistols in his coat pockets, just in case, although no evidence exists that he ever used them. Nonetheless, he earned a good reputation as a fair and decisive judge and was well-respected among the people in the area. Within a year he was elected to California's first state legislature, where he served until 1857 when he was elected to the California Supreme Court. Field would serve on that court until 1863, with three of those six years as Chief Justice. It was during this time on the court in California that the forty-three year old Field met and married his life mate, Sue Virginia Sweringen.

At the expiration of his state Supreme Court term, Field was appointed by President Abraham Lincoln to the United States Supreme Court, to the new "tenth seat"

---

[27] Spanish word, pronounced (all-CALL-day)

that had been created by Congress. It would later be abolished after the death of Justice John Catron in 1865. The Republican Lincoln nominated the generally conservative Unionist Democrat in order to create a regional balance on the Court, with Field coming essentially from the west and bringing experience in real estate and mining issues. Williams College bestowed honorary Master of Arts and Doctor of Laws degrees upon him a year after taking his seat on the Court. He received yet another honorary Doctorate degree from the University of California in 1869.

While on the Court, Field consistently upheld the interests of businesses and private property rights and also fought to have the federal income tax abolished. In 1877, he sat in as a member of and voted with the Democratic minority in the Hayes-Tilden electoral commission. This commission's decision essentially decided the election of 1876 that gave the White House to Rutherford B. Hayes. Four years later, Field himself would seek out the Democratic presidential nomination. Perhaps it was just as well that he was unsuccessful at the Democratic National Convention. For if he had received the nomination, he would have been pitted against the Republican nominee who ended up winning the presidency, his Williams Chapter Fraternity brother, James A. Garfield, *Williams 1856*. This certainly could have made for an interesting decision for Delta Upsilon voters!

Although certainly married to his profession, Field still maintained an interest in the affairs of the Fraternity. In 1884, although not in attendance, he agreed to have his name appear as the Honorary President of the Fiftieth Convention of the Fraternity, held in New York

City. This showed, at least, that Field continued to feel strong affinity for the Fraternity.

In 1888, Field returned to California during the Supreme Court's break to hear cases as the senior justice in the California federal courts, as the Supreme Court justices would do at that time. While there, he heard a very interesting appeal case. A young woman had been divorced from a local millionaire and had tried to claim part of his fortune. She had lost her case and eventually married former Chief Justice of the California Supreme Court, David S. Terry. Known for his fiery temper, Terry had killed his once close friend Senator David Broderick in a duel. Terry claimed that Broderick had engineered Terry's re-election defeat for the court in 1859. After his forced retirement from the court, Terry challenged Broderick to a duel. After Broderick's pistol misfired, Terry shot Broderick, who died three days later. Broderick, also, had been a close friend of Judge Stephen J. Field.

Fast forwarding thirty years, David Terry and his new wife now found themselves in Field's court for their appeal. Field not only ruled against them, but jailed them both for contempt of court after they protested Field's judicial decision. Terry vowed to get even.

Once out of jail, Terry boarded a train on August 14, 1889 that was headed to San Francisco. By sheer coincidence, the train also carried Justice Field and his bodyguard. Field had actually expected a possible encounter with Terry while in California, but went about his activities without the least bit of concern, saying it was both his duty and pleasure to sustain the dignity of the bench, despite the possible trouble that might await him. Terry noticed Field on the train, and his blood began to boil. While at a dining stop at the station restaurant in Lathrop, California, Terry approached Field and slapped him twice across the face. Field's bodyguard reacted immediately and shot Terry once, killing him instantly.

Field would indirectly make history again as being the only person in the history of the United States to have his nephew join him on the Supreme Court. On January 6, 1890, Justice David Brewer assumed the high court after being nominated by President Benjamin Harrison. Brewer was the son of Stephen's eldest sister Emelia, with whom he had traveled to Turkey sixty years before.

By 1896, the eighty year-old Field began to show signs of age and occasional senility. His colleagues on the court began to urge Field to retire, telling him that he could have retired on full pay ten years before. However, Field had long ago made a resolution never to die nor resign while Democratic president Grover Cleveland was in office.
Field believed that he had been insulted by the President when Cleveland did not appoint him Chief Justice upon the death of Morrison Waite, despite the fact that Field felt that Cleveland owed him some political debts. Cleveland appointed Melville Fuller as Chief Justice instead. From that point on Field refused to set foot in the White House while Cleveland was in office. Field preferred to continue working, at least until Cleveland was gone, and also insisted on breaking the record of continuous years of service on the court, held by former Chief Justice John Marshall. Even though Field was a Democrat, he also felt that having

been named to the court by a Republican president; he owed it to a future Republican president to name his successor.

In August of 1897, Field broke Justice Marshall's record of service on the Supreme Court bench. Nearly eighty-one, his mind was mostly still sharp despite the words of his critics, but his body was wearing out. He had realized his goal of becoming the new judicial record holder with more than thirty four years and seven months of service on the United States Supreme Court. And, since new Republican president, William McKinley, had taken office, Field finally relented and announced his retirement from the Court. Field retired on December 1, 1897, bringing an end to one of the most storied careers in the history of the High Court. His record would stand for over seventy-five years until Justice William O. Douglas broke Field's record in 1973, eventually surpassing it by more than two years.

Field retired to his home in Washington, D.C. with his wife to live out the remainder of his days, which would not be many. Just sixteen months after his retirement, the venerable justice passed away at his home, surrounded by his wife, nephew and a few friends.

Resolutions were received from the Supreme Court and several other courts from around the country, lamenting the death of the noted jurist. After a brief prayer service at Field's home, a small, private and unostentatious funeral was held at the Episcopal Church of the Epiphany in Washington, D.C., where Field had been a member for more than thirty years. The only hint that the remains of the deceased were of anyone important, was that the honorary pallbearers were the Chief Justice and the eight Associate Justices of the United States. After the brief church service, the interment services were private, attended only by family, intimate friends and the Supreme Court justices. He was laid to rest in the Rock Creek Cemetery in Washington, D.C., where many of the nation's notable and historical citizens are buried.

Lewis Conger Lockwood
Williams 1837

REV. LEWIS CONGER LOCKWOOD '37
"The Last Brother"

Born: December 20, 1815
Died: December 1, 1904 (Age 88)
Buried: Riverhead Cemetery
                     Riverhead, NY (Long Island)
Marriage: 1852
                     Huldah Terry (d. 2/3/1907)
Children: One
Occupation: Minister
Dorm Room: 13 West College

Lewis Conger Lockwood earns the title "The Last Brother" as being the sole survivor, the last one standing, and the one to outlive all of the other Founders. It is somewhat ironic that he was also one of the first to take a stand.

Born in New Windsor, New York on December 20, 1815, Lewis Conger Lockwood was one of five of Delta Upsilon's thirty Founders to <u>not</u> graduate from Williams College. After enrolling at Williams, he spent two years studying in addition to playing an active role in the Founding of the Society. He is documented as being one of the "early men"; the ones who made the decision to start the group and recruit other like minded individuals.

Lockwood studied at Williams for only two years, beginning in 1834, which makes it even more special that he jumped on the non-secret bandwagon so soon. Arguably, he would not have had the same amount of time to witness the secret oppression that had

overtaken the Williams campus. But apparently
something inside him knew that a change was needed,
and he quickly joined forces with those who decided to
move into action.

How he got connected in the beginning is unknown. He
lived in room thirteen of West College, between the
rooms of Noble and Sparks in room twelve and Page in
room fourteen. Brown and Lyman were two doors down
in room eleven. So he certainly had company, and likely
heard the rumblings. Regardless, he sympathized with
the effort quickly and would become one of the early
spiritual leaders of the group. What is certain is that he
was in Room Twenty-Two of East College with Tappan
and Field to discuss the non-secret idea.

After the Founding, he carried on until about 1836,
when he transferred out of Williams to Union College in
Schenectady, New York where he completed his
education and graduated in 1838. Transferring to
Union would prove to set a precedent. After his
graduation from Union, he enrolled and spent the 1838-
39 school year at the Princeton Theological Seminary in
Princeton, New Jersey. For the following 1839-40 school
year he transferred to the newly founded Union
Theological Seminary in New York City, only to return
to the Princeton Seminary for the 1840-41 school year.
By that time, the issue of slavery had been a topic of
discussion for several years. Lockwood took a keen
interest in this and began to sympathize with the
abolitionist movement.

In 1834, one of the first major public discussions of
slavery took place, which resulted in nothing less than
an anti-slavery revival at the Lane Theological

Seminary in Cincinnati, Ohio.[28] Given his growing interest and feelings of attachment for the anti-slavery movement, he later transferred to Lane for his final year of study, where he graduated in 1842.

That same year he was ordained in Cincinnati, Ohio. He preached briefly in Reading, Ohio before moving back to New England to fill various pastorates at churches in New York and Connecticut until 1860. During that time, from 1852 to 1854, he held a pastorate in New York City. It was there that the thirty-seven year old bachelor pastor met and subsequently married his nineteen year old bride, Miss Huldah Terry, of Aquebogue, Long Island, New York. On March 15, 1859, Lewis and Huldah would welcome their only child, their daughter Carrie.

Following Carrie's birth, Lockwood helped organize both the New York Emigrant Aid Society and the New York Army Commission. By 1861, he was serving as Chaplain of the Christian Commission during the Civil War. It was during this time as Chaplain that he would finally put his sympathy towards abolitionism into action.

He traveled to Washington, D.C. to meet with government officials and military leaders about the idea of establishing a Freedmen's School in Hampton, Virginia. The somewhat surprising result of those meetings (for the time) was the encouragement of the government and the recommendation of the

---

[28] Known for the famous "Lane Debates" that occurred in 1834, the Seminary operated from 1829 to about 1932 when it became part of the McCormick Theological Seminary in Chicago, Illinois.

commanding officer, General John E. Wool, who had secured nearby Fort Monroe for the Union Army as an asylum for escaped slaves. General Wool assured Reverend Lockwood of his full support and promised his assistance in providing whatever might be needed to start the effort.

Lockwood returned to Hampton and conferred with the leaders among the freedmen. He investigated the condition and desires of the people, and then subsequently made arrangements for weekday and Sabbath meetings and organized weekday and evening schools. He employed several of the most intelligent and gifted freedmen as assistants, and arranged to collect additional clothing for them, as well as for other missionaries and teachers.

The first teacher employed was Mrs. Mary S. Peake, a free black citizen of the Commonwealth of Virginia, who began teaching under the shade of a broad oak tree at the newly formed Freedmen's School. Despite contracting tuberculosis, Mrs. Peake was a tireless worker and teacher, and Reverend Lockwood respected her greatly. She continued to teach as long as her health permitted, but passed away on Washington's Birthday in 1862. The following year, 1863, the first southern reading of President Lincoln's Emancipation Proclamation would occur underneath the very tree where Mrs. Peake began her teaching. That same tree, today, is known as the famous "Emancipation Oak" on the grounds of the former Freedman's School, later renamed the Hampton Institute, and now known as the current Hampton University.

Lockwood would continue to serve as a missionary at the school until 1865, after the Civil War had ended. But almost immediately upon the death of Mrs. Peake, he began writing her memoirs to help perpetuate her memory. <u>Mary S. Peake: The Colored Teacher at Fortress Monroe</u> is one of several books written by Lockwood.[29]

For the next twenty years, he split time between two churches in New York, serving for nine years in Brooklyn and at another pastorate in Melville for eleven years, before leaving the ministry in 1885 to retire to his home in Woodhaven, New York on Long Island. On October 4, 1889, the Lockwood's daughter Carrie, who had lived with them her entire life, passed away unexpectedly at age thirty.

By 1903, Lewis Lockwood and Francis Tappan were the last two living Founders. It is ironic that they were, arguably, two of the first who started the Social Fraternity nearly seventy years before. The Fraternity's leadership had invited both of the Founders to attend the Fraternity's Sixty-Ninth Anniversary Convention in 1903, held in New York City. Showing his continued interest in the Fraternity by his reply, he sent this message on November 10, 1903:

---

[29] *Lockwood's book, <u>Mary S. Peake: the Colored Teacher at Fortress Monroe</u> is available online as a free E-book. To gain further insight into Lockwood's admiration for this extraordinary woman, visit <u>http://www.gutenberg.org/etext/20744</u> to download a free e-book copy.*

"Dear Brother:

Your invitation to attend the meeting of the Delta Upsilon Fraternity is highly appreciated. As one of its Founders, I would be very glad to attend the convention, and especially to participate in the banquet on Friday evening. But, being now near the close of the 88th year of my age, it would be physically indiscreet, if not impracticable. You have my best wishes for an enjoyable entertainment.

Yours Fraternally,

Lewis C. Lockwood, Williams '37"

Eleven months passed, and on October 31, 1904, the only other remaining Founder, Francis Tappan, passed away, leaving Lockwood as the only Founder to even witness the Seventieth Anniversary of the Fraternity, five days later on November 4, 1904.

His title as the "only living Founder" would not last long. Just three weeks before his eighty-ninth birthday, he passed away at his home on Long Island on December 1, 1904, just one month after Judge Tappan, forever closing the chapter on the lives of the Fraternity's Founders.

Lewis Lockwood was laid to rest in the Riverhead Cemetery in Riverhead, New York, next to his daughter, Carrie. His wife, Huldah would only survive another two years, even though she was nearly twenty years his junior.

The last photo taken of Lewis Lockwood
in September of 1904, just three
months before his death.

Dear Brother Goldsmith
I enjoyed the Delta upsilon
Magazine, that you sent to me
Very much and thank you
for your kind offer to place me
on the subscription list free from
Charge. I shall gladly welcome you
as a visitor whenever you may
find it convenient to call

Yours fraternally
Lewis C. Lockwood

A copy of a letter, in Lockwood's own hand, thanking
then-editor of the *Delta Upsilon Quarterly* magazine,
Goldwyn Goldsmith, *Columbia 1896*, for a free lifetime
subscription to the *Quarterly*.

DR. LYNDON GRAVES LYMAN '37
"The Dentist"

Born:	June 14, 1810
Died:	September 4, 1871 (Age 61)
Buried:	Evergreen Cemetery
	Hillside, New Jersey
Marriage:	July 28, 1844
	Mary Castner (d. 1847)
Children:	Two
Marriage:	January 12, 1853
	Jane Robb (d. 5/6/1900)
Children:	Five
Occupation:	Dentist
Dorm Room:	11 West College

The youngest of the twelve children of Deacon Aaron Lyman and Electa Graves Lyman, and one of only two of their four sons to live into adulthood, Lyndon Lyman was born in Charlemont, Massachusetts on June 14, 1810.

Of the early life of Lyndon Lyman, nothing is known. His story here begins in 1833, when he left his large family and enrolled at Williams College. He associated easily with the efforts of the new non-secret fraternity, joining together with his roommate, Daniel Brown.

Lyndon would associate with the new Social Fraternity only for a short time however, staying only one year beyond the November Founding and opting to leave Williams after the fall semester in 1835.

He was one of only five Founders to not graduate from Williams. It is apparent that he left Williams

143

immediately for New Jersey, perhaps to continue his education or perhaps to "find himself". Regardless, what he did is still a mystery. The most probable scenario is that after moving to Newark in 1835, he began to pursue the relatively new profession of dentistry. The world's first dental school in America, the Baltimore College of Dental Surgery, opened in 1840, a relatively short distance away from Newark. Regardless, he apparently did earn his doctoral degree in dental surgery and returned to Newark to practice dentistry, joining Anson Hobart as one of the two Founders to pursue a career in medicine.

On July 28, 1844, he married Mary Castner of Washington, New Jersey. He and Mary started a family with the birth of their first daughter, Emma, who arrived December 8, 1845. Her sister, Mary, joined the family on October 5, 1847. Mary was a strong and healthy girl, but the birth was apparently a tough one for her mother. On October 16, just eleven days after giving birth to her namesake, Lyndon's wife, Mary, passed away. Now a widower, Lyndon made his way with his two young daughters and his growing dental practice.

On January 12, 1853, just over five years after the death of his first wife, Lyndon married Jane Robb of Newark. He and Jane would expand the Lyman family and have five children together. Elizabeth and Anna were born in 1854 and 1855, respectively. Anna, however, would not even survive a year, passing away just after turning eleven months old. A year and a half later their only son, William, was born in 1858, followed by daughters, Jennie (1860) and Julia (1865). Lyndon would support this large brood with a successful dental

144

practice that became more widely accepted with the growing development and acceptance of the profession. His practice operated in the same building as his home at 886 Broad Street in Newark, with the family living on the upper floors of the building.

From the lack of information, correspondence and fraternal record, Lyndon Lyman was clearly focused on family and profession. His connection to the Fraternity continued to exist after his departure from Williams, but only in the form of brief updates regarding his whereabouts.

By 1870, the sixty year old dentist had developed a tumor in his body that eventually claimed his life on September 4, 1871. After a funeral held at his home and attended by numerous family and friends, Brother Lyman was laid to rest in Evergreen Cemetery, next to his father-in-law, John Robb.

Jane Lyman would eventually remarry, exchanging vows with Thomas McKee in 1874. Their twelve year marriage would end upon McKee's death in 1886. Jane Robb Lyman McKee would be buried between both of her husbands upon her own death in 1900.

Lyndon Lyman was buried two months before the birth of notable Red Badge of Courage author Stephen Crane, *Lafayette & Syracuse 1894,* who would join the fraternity that Lyman began sixty years before. Crane himself would be buried just one month after Lyman's wife Jane, and ironically, just a few yards away in the same section of Evergreen Cemetery.

Photo of what was once the Lyman home and dental
office at then 886 Broad Street in Newark, New Jersey.
Today it is a retail building.
(White bricked portion at far left)

HENRY MORGAN '37
"The Judge"

Born:	January 8, 1814
Died:	January 8, 1894 (Age 80)
Buried:	Oakview Cemetery
	Albany, Georgia
Marriage:	None
Children:	None
Occupation:	Attorney, Judge
Dorm Room:	17 West College

Surprisingly, we do not know as much as we should about a man who was both successful and in the public eye. On January 8, 1814, Henry Morgan entered this world in the town of Stockbridge, Massachusetts. At the age of nineteen, he and his best friend from Stockbridge entered Williams College together for the 1833 school year to study and prepare for their yet undecided careers. Intelligent, diligent and a well-rounded student, he was a natural fit for the Social Fraternity in its beginnings. Morgan was likely very strongly influenced to join the Fraternity by Stephen Field and Edward Clarke who had been his friends in Stockbridge. Shortly after the Founding, Morgan recruited his best friend and roommate, George Turner, to join the Fraternity as well.

However, Morgan's time with the group would prove to be short. In 1835, he left Williams College for good and eventually traveled south to Georgia. What took him to Georgia is unknown, but he nonetheless settled in the town of Americus and began teaching in 1836. He taught grade school in Americus through 1837, a year before moving to Palmyra, Georgia, where he taught for another two years.

Apparently deciding that teaching was not to be his lifelong profession, he began to work in the field of journalism. In 1841, he joined forces with a friend, N.W. Collier, and the two became founders and editors of the *Southwestern Georgian* in Albany, Georgia. On May 25, 1841, they published their first issue. The weekly newspaper was the first newspaper to be published in Albany and was neutral in politics. "It did much to remove the false opinions and strong prejudices of the people in the older sections of the state, in regard to the diseases and health of Southwestern Georgia, which was then, by some, regarded as a graveyard."[30]

Perhaps after some soul searching, Henry entered Law School in 1842, where he studied for three years and continued work on the paper. In 1845, he left the journalism business for good. He was admitted to the Georgia State Bar and began a new career as a practicing attorney, a career that would encompass the next twenty-three years. In 1865, Morgan represented Dougherty County at the Georgia Constitutional Convention, which met in accordance with instructions from U.S. President Andrew Johnson. It was at this Convention that Georgia adopted a new state Constitution, officially abolishing slavery in the state. Serving in this capacity gave Morgan a taste for further public service. In 1868 he was elected in his own right to the Georgia State House of Representatives, but would serve only one term before being unseated in 1870. On January 1, 1871, his career vision became a reality as

---

[30] From the <u>Historical Background of Dougherty County: 1836-1940</u>

he was appointed to be the presiding Judge of Georgia's Tenth Senatorial District Court. Morgan could no doubt see himself in this job until his retirement. But this position, unfortunately, would be even shorter than his State congressional career. Due to the redrawing of the district lines, the court was abruptly abolished on December 7, 1871, with all pending cases being transferred to the superior court. Not even a full year into his dream job, Morgan was again defeated.

Undeterred, he went back to his life's work and continued his law practice in Albany, Georgia well into the 1880s. But despite his successes and high profile positions, Morgan was undoubtedly lonely. He had friends, certainly, but lived in boarding houses virtually his entire life, never married and had no children. What family he had left, if any, was still in New England. Being a driven and successful attorney among other things, he may have preferred it that way, focusing on his career instead of other things.

On January 8, 1894, Henry Morgan passed away, alone, on his eightieth birthday.

The sad story does not end there, however.

Henry Morgan was laid to rest in Oakview Cemetery in Albany, Georgia the day after his death. One hundred years later, in July of 1994, Tropical Storm Alberto ravaged and devastated southern Georgia. Most consider it the worst natural disaster to ever hit the state. Alberto hung over the state for several days, dumping nearly thirty inches of water in some areas. Albany was one of the most affected areas. The Flint River rose over twenty feet above its normal flood stage.

Thousands of homes and many schools were destroyed. Also affected were the two largest cemeteries in town, one of which was Oakview.

Headstones were washed away, some of which were never found. Markers, tombs and other landmarks that were there when the water rose, had disappeared by the time the water receded. The cemetery office flooded, and a great number of their burial records were destroyed. As for the burial marker and record for Henry Morgan, neither appears to have survived.

Morgan rests at Oakview, somewhere. His whereabouts are now a victim of Mother Nature, and lost to the ages. Fortunately we know a little about the man who voted for the abolition of slavery in Georgia, and who saw justice prevailed in the court of law, if even for a short time. More than that, we know a little about a person who stood up for non-secrecy by founding a Fraternity, and asking his best friend to join.

WILLIAM HENRY NOBLE '37
"The Engineer"

Born: May 22, 1817
Died: May 13, 1867 (Age 49)
Buried: Green Ridge Cemetery
                    Kenosha, Wisconsin
Marriage: 1847
                    Jenny Orr
Children: None
Occupation: Teacher, Civil Engineer, Editor
Dorm Room: 12 West College

Before telling the story of William Henry Noble, one must surely read about his father, the Honorable Daniel Noble.

Daniel Noble was born a citizen of the United States of America, barely. He was born in Williamstown, Massachusetts on July 7, 1776, just three days after the Second Continental Congress adopted the resolution for Independence from Britain. He grew up in Williamstown, and in 1796 at the age of twenty, he graduated from Williams College, which had just been formed three years earlier.

After studying law in Williamstown under the guidance of a local lawyer, Daniel Noble set out to practice in the town of South Adams, where he married his wife, Esther, in 1802. In 1811, he returned to his native Williamstown to practice law and began serving as a Trustee of Williams College, the first Williams alumnus to do so. In 1814, he became Treasurer of the college. On May 22, 1817, he and Esther welcomed a child into the world and appropriately named him William.

Daniel Noble was a member of both branches of the state government and was once a candidate for Lieutenant Governor of Massachusetts. He was a student of religion as well and was described as being a very pious man. In 1820, while serving as Treasurer, he opposed a measure by the President of the college to move Williams College to Northampton, Massachusetts and threw his entire effort and influence into support of the opposition. The result of his effort was the defeat of the measure that was already highly supported by the college president and a large majority of its Trustees. Had it not been for Daniel Noble the college undoubtedly would have been moved. Essentially, the reason that Williams College still exists where it is today is thanks to Daniel Noble.

As a proud alumnus of Williams, it was only fitting to Daniel that his son, William Henry (along with William's younger brother Solomon) would also enroll at the college. One might guess that his father and grandfather, who was also a big supporter of the college, might have said that "Williams College was William's College."

William Henry Noble was born in Williamstown, Massachusetts, the only Founding Father to claim that fact. He was also the only one of the Founders to engage in the study of civil engineering. In his early life he became associated with the church and is said to have maintained a "consistent Christian character" throughout his life. He was described as possessing "an uncommon degree of urbanity and gentleness of manners, with kindness of heart, which won the love of all who knew him." His work ethic was strong, and he possessed a strong passion for his profession. He was said to be "full of energy, industry and perseverance, and brought out results and reports of much value and importance."[31]

After his graduation from Williams, he taught for several years before moving into practice of his chosen profession. He worked for a time building railroads in Maine, Pennsylvania and Ohio. While in Maine, in 1847, he married Jenny Orr, the daughter of U.S. Congressman Benjamin Orr.

In the 1850s, Noble began consulting on the project to construct the Boston Cochituate Water Works. He also joined a Masonic Lodge, dedicating what little spare time he had. His tireless work and the long hours he kept eventually affected his health and forced him to alter his career. He began working with the *National Merchant*, a newspaper published in Burlington, Iowa, and would often travel as a result of his job between there and the home that he had established in Kenosha, Wisconsin.

On Monday morning, May 13, 1867, in the course of his business travel, he boarded the *Lansing*, a small stern-wheel steamboat that was operated on the Mississippi River and leased by the Western Union Railroad Company to run in connection with their trains between Rock Island and Port Byron, Illinois. At 8:30 am as scheduled, the boat left the levee at Rock Island for her short trip upriver with a stop in Hampton, Illinois to take on wood to heat the boilers and to take on additional passengers.

---

[31] Both quotes from the <u>Williams College Biographical Annals</u>

Upon arrival at Hampton, a strong west wind prevailed, which caused the boat to become "wind-bound" and run into the landing at Hampton. With the captain at the wheel, the boat hands and some of the passengers stood on the stern of the boat attempting to push the *Lansing* away from shore and get the boat underway, which was difficult at best fighting those high winds. No doubt that Noble, with his experience as a civil engineer and troubleshooter, was an active participant in trying to find a solution to this dilemma. During the effort, the boat's engineer had allegedly hung a large wrench on the safety valve of the boat's boilers, which slowly tightened and built up more steam than the boilers could stand as the boat rocked and bobbed.

Around noon, after more than three hours of trying to push the boat off shore, the boiler on the shore side of the boat suddenly exploded out and towards the shore, destroying the bow of the boat, leaving the stern of the boat and those standing on that end, virtually untouched.

The explosion was of such force that the steam chest and other heavy debris from the ship were found over a quarter mile away. One of the several injured survivors was blown into a vacant lot over four-hundred feet away. The bodies of the victims were mangled and scalded and the pilot of the boat was found on shore with the spokes of the pilot wheel driven through his body. Two other members of the boat's crew were killed, along with the three passengers who had been assisting in the effort to free the boat from shore.

Photograph of the Steamer Lansing, taken
the afternoon of the explosion.

One of the victims of this terrible accident was Delta
Upsilon Founder William Henry Noble.

The citizens of Hampton opened their homes to the
survivors and attended to the wounded along with Dr.
Vincent, the only local doctor in the area. At the same
time, an inquest was held over the bodies of the victims.

William Henry Noble's body was returned to Kenosha,
Wisconsin, to his surviving wife and many friends left to
mourn him. Williamstown's native son was buried ten
days after the accident with Masonic honors at Green
Ridge Cemetery in Kenosha, Wisconsin in a cemetery
plot provided by Stephen Jackson, a brother in his
Masonic Lodge.

COMFORT SPARKS '37
"His Father's Son"

Born:	1813
Died:	October 3, 1838 (Age 25)
Buried:	Bow Wow Cemetery
	Sheffield, Massachusetts
Marriage:	None
Children:	None
Occupation:	Teacher
Dorm Room:	11 West College

Of all of the Founders of the Fraternity, the least is known about Comfort Sparks. He was the son of Deacon Comfort and Asemath Sparks, of Mount Washington Township in Berkshire County, Massachusetts. With his father a leader in the church, he himself became a member of the Congregational Church in Sheffield in July of 1831.

He undoubtedly joined the Fraternity together with his roommate William Noble. Immediately after graduating from Williams he became a teacher and taught school in Lanesboro, Massachusetts, while preparing to enter the ministry. It was there in Lanesboro where he died, October 3, 1838, at the age of twenty-five. His body was brought back to Sheffield where he was buried in the family plot in what is now known as the Bow Wow Cemetery, well off the beaten path in Sheffield.

Francis Wilder Tappan
Williams 1837

158

FRANCIS WILDER TAPPAN '37
"The Youngest Brother"

Born:	December 29, 1817
Died:	October 31, 1904 (Age 86)
Buried:	Riverside Cemetery
	Fairhaven, Massachusetts
Marriage:	December 20, 1843
	Belinda L. DePeyster (d. 1907)
Children:	Three
Occupation:	Attorney / District Court Judge
Dorm Room:	22 East College

Francis Wilder Tappan was the only city boy in the bunch, having been born in Boston, Massachusetts on December 29, 1817, making him the youngest of the Founding Fathers. He was but seven months younger than William Henry Noble, and over a year younger than Stephen J. Field. All of the remaining Founders, even those behind him in the Class of 1838, were from two to eleven years his senior.

He was "number seven" in a line of the twelve children of John and Sarah Tappan. He prepared for college in Boston before crossing the state to attend college at Williams. He was just fifteen years old when a professor from Williams College visited the Tappan homestead in Boston. The College, for some reason, wanted to gain the influence of Francis' father. The visiting professor suggested to Francis' father that Francis should be sent to college, with the professor even offering to provide shelter for the young boy. Mr. Tappan accepted the offer and Francis headed west towards Williamstown, testing in as a sophomore in May 1834.

159

Despite his young age, Francis proved his maturity by showing his readiness for higher education and not being the least bit intimidated by the thought of associating himself with students already much older than he. While at Williams, he quickly connected not only with his classmates, but with many of the upperclassmen, with whom he shared similar views. Part of this association was due, in part, to the fact that he was one of only two sophomores that were housed in East College, normally reserved for juniors and seniors.

It was during this time that Tappan and his classmates witnessed "the evils of the secret societies" on the Williams campus and set out to have the opposite influence. The idea of the formation of a non-secret society was first suggested and discussed among some classmates in an organizational meeting held in Tappan's room in East College. Following this meeting, Tappan, the main link between the juniors and those in his own class of sophomores, would carry the message of the formation of this non-secret group over to West College during his daily academic routine, slowly but certainly influencing those in the sophomore and freshman classes.

After graduating from Williams in 1837, he studied law both in New York City, and with the Honorable Judge Daniel Cady in Johnstown, New York. He traveled extensively in Europe throughout 1839 and 1840 and then returned to the United States, where he settled in Ravenna, Ohio to practice law. On December 20, 1843, he married Belinda DePeyster, the daughter of Judge George B. DePeyster in Portage, Ohio. Four years later they had a son, Francis DePeyster Tappan, born March

2, 1847. Another son, Lewis Henry, would follow on September 24, 1851, but would not live a full year.

Francis and Belinda stayed in Ravenna until 1853, when ill health forced a change of scenery back to the air of the eastern shore. He headed back east with his wife and son, settling in the area of Burlington, New Jersey, between Philadelphia and New York. In 1854, their daughter Martha Elizabeth (affectionately referred to as "Mattie") was born. Time would not be kind to Mattie either, who passed away just after her second birthday in 1856, as was the case for many children of this era.

For the next sixteen years, Francis Tappan was in business with commercial and collecting agencies in Philadelphia and New York City. In 1866, their son, Francis, presented them with their first grandchild, their grandson, Lewis. Their subsequent two grandchildren would not survive infancy either, so they doted on Lewis for the remainder of their lives.

In 1869, Tappan returned to Massachusetts to set up a real estate and law office at 15 North Water Street in New Bedford, making the short daily commute from his home in Fairhaven. In about 1875, he became the Special Justice for the Third District Court of Bristol County and obtained the title of "Judge", by which he would be referred for the rest of his life.

On July 4, 1895, while most people were celebrating the birth of the United States, Francis and Belinda were lamenting the death of their last living child, Francis, who passed away at age forty-six.

The Tappan Law Office in New Bedford, Massachusetts

By this time, their grandson Lewis had moved back to Ohio, married, and made Francis and Belinda great-grandparents three times over.

After his retirement, Tappan and Belinda spent the remainder of their days at their home at 14 Fort Street, high on a hill directly across from New Bedford, near the end of the point on which Fort Phoenix stood.[32] They lived out their days by rarely going out, but more often just sitting on the porch, enjoying the view overlooking the Acushnet River and Buzzard's Bay.

---

[32] In 1904, their home was the last house before the point. Other homes have since been built closer to the point. Fort Phoenix was the site of the first naval battle of the Revolutionary War in 1775.

The Tappan Home in Fairhaven, Massachusetts

By 1901, Tappan was one of only three Founders to see the twentieth century. He remained, however, a proud and loyal son of Delta Upsilon. He, like Lewis Lockwood was invited to attend the sixty-ninth DU Convention in New York City in 1903, but sent this regret on November 3, 1903:

"Dear Brother:

I am deeply affected by your fraternal invitation to the sixty-ninth Convention of the Delta Upsilon Fraternity in New York City. I am thereby reminded that I am one of the few of the Founders of the Social Fraternity in Williams College in 1834, selected from the classes of 1837 and 1838, and that this fact has prompted this invitation so kindly expressed.

It is with sincere regret that I must say to you that the infirmities of my advanced age, now almost eighty-six years, forbid my acceptance of the invitation and, therefore, I must be denied the enjoyment of the festive occasion.

When I recall the beneficial effects of the Fraternity upon its members, and when I contemplate the numerous chapters subsequently formed, I am impressed with the belief that the Divine Master, who brought to Williamstown the men who constituted the praying band at the Hay Stack,[33] whom He inspired to consecrate themselves to the great work of foreign missions, sent to Williams College the proper men to found the Social Fraternity that was to help in the

---

[33] The Haystack Monument on the campus of Williams College marks birthplace of American Foreign Missions. The site was where, in 1806, five students met for a prayer meeting in the lee of a large haystack and effectively spurned the development of Protestant Missions.

education of students in the various colleges of the
United States.

   Again thanking you and your associates for the
attention to me, at this time, I remain,

Yours Fraternally,

Francis Wilder Tappan, Williams '37

Francis Wilder Tappan, one of the first organizers of the
Fraternity, was one of two remaining Founders when he
passed away at his home in Fairhaven on October 31,
1904, just five days before the Seventieth Anniversary
of the Fraternity. He was outlived by fellow Founder
Lewis Lockwood by only one month.

On November 2, 1904, Francis Tappan was laid to rest
near his children in the family plot in Riverside
Cemetery and was joined three years later by his
beloved wife, Belinda.

The last known photo of Francis Tappan, sitting on his porch with his wife Belinda in 1904.

The Class of 1838

Willard Brigham

Edward Flint Brooks

William Bross

Thomas Amory Hall

John Peabody Hills

Foster Lilly

Theophilus Page

Charles Peabody

David Pise

Francis Williams

The Freshmen

The class of 1838, or "the third ten of one of the three lower classes" at Williams in November of 1834, contains some of the steadiest members of each of the three classes. In this class, one would find the Founder who was arguably the most intriguing and eccentric character of all of them combined. One would also find a teacher of a future U.S. President, and the one member who was the most active in Delta Upsilon after his graduation.

The freshman class could also be called "the class of eighty". Eighty percent of this class graduated from Williams. Like the juniors, eighty percent of the members of the class were ministers. All of them, whether ministers or not, held to some religious belief, and each with their own unique life story. And, we only know the "whereabouts" of eight of ten freshmen – again, eighty percent.

The freshman class would produce eight ministers, a merchant, and a man of great distinction who lived a full life in journalism and politics. This class had the highest rate of longevity, despite the fact that two of them died in the 1850s. The rest made it at least to age sixty (save one who missed that mark by two weeks), with five of the ten living well into the 1890s.

Of these ten, seven of them (referred to as the "freshman seven") were "huddled" in a short radius of each other within the freshman dorm, meaning, each of their rooms was relatively adjacent to one another.

Hence, recruitment was perhaps easier and joining was almost a given for the men on this dorm floor. However, they were hardly followers. They were arguably the most studious and serious of the three classes and held to a quiet consistency that helped to steady the entire group. In a sense they, as freshmen, were being groomed for future leadership roles, with the third and fourth chapter presidents coming from this group. They were the keel that kept this non-secret ship upright and balanced.

They bought into the effort of non-secrecy from the very beginning, and suffered the slurs and epithets on "day two" like the rest of the Founders. They were the ones who were counted on by the two previous classes, to continue forward with the cause of justice, to ensure that the organization lived on...and they delivered.

They were...the torch bearers...

REV. WILLARD BRIGHAM '38
"The Minister"

Born:	May 4, 1813
Died:	March 2, 1874 (Age 60)
Buried:	Riverside Cemetery
	Winchendon, Massachusetts
Marriage:	May 4, 1843
	Maria Davenport (d. 1857)
Marriage:	October 2, 1860
	Laura Cleveland (d. 1/15/1889)
Children:	Four
Occupation:	Teacher, Minister
Dorm Room:	5 West College

In 1813, Marlborough, Massachusetts was a favorite stop for traveling on the Boston Post Road, the major "highway" or postal route in those days, from Boston to New York City. A small but growing town, Marlborough boasted a number of inns and taverns, frequented by travelers, including George Washington, who visited after his inauguration in 1789. It was also the site on May 4, 1813, of the birth of Willard Brigham, the sixth of the eight children of Willard Sr. and Betsey Brigham.

Willard Brigham enrolled at Williams to begin the fall term in 1834. Like most of the freshmen, he lived in the lower of the floors of West College, in Room Five. Seven of the ten residents of the second floor dorm rooms, one through five, joined the Social Fraternity at its beginning. He was, by nature, a congenial person and was no doubt sympathetic, but more so, was willing to offer a helping hand to this group of men who formed this new organization for fair play.

171

While in college, he would listen to stories about New Hampshire and the areas in northern Massachusetts from his roommate, Labian Sherman, who hailed from Manchester, New Hampshire. Wanting to give the area a try, Brigham headed north to that area following his graduation in 1838, settling in Pepperell, Massachusetts, just a stone's throw from the New Hampshire border.

He began teaching at an academy in Pepperell upon his arrival, but taught there only a year. Feeling the call to the ministry, he left Pepperell and entered the Andover Theological School[34] at Andover, Massachusetts, where he studied for the next three years. After the completion of his studies at Andover, he was called to Wardsboro, Vermont to begin his life as a minister. It was during this time that he caught the eye of Miss Maria Davenport of Royalton. After a suitable courtship, Willard and Maria were married on May 4, 1843. Three weeks later, on May 24, he was ordained at North Wardsboro where he would stay and preach for twelve years, until the end of 1855.

While in Vermont, Willard and Maria would raise a family of four children: daughter, Helen (1844), son, Albert (1847), son, Herbert (1849) and daughter, Mary (1855), the latter named after his favorite sister.

At the start of 1856, they would move back to his beloved Bay State and begin a twelve year transient period, ministering for seven years in Ashfield, followed by three years in Wendell. However, in 1857, after his

---

[34] Now Andover Newton Theological Seminary

first year in Ashfield, his beloved wife, Maria, passed away. Devastated but faithful, he carried on without her, focusing on his children and his life's work. While at Ashfield, he would not only recover from his loss, but would marry again, on October 23, 1860, to Laura Cleveland, who had moved there from Medfield.

The final two years of his "transient" period were spent in Wellfleet, Massachusetts, halfway between the tip and the "elbow" of Cape Cod. Certainly a departure from the "middle northern" part of Massachusetts that he was used to, he hurried back to his more familiar surroundings in 1868, finally settling for good in Winchendon.

For the next six years, he continued to preach in Winchendon as his adult children began to make lives of their own. Willard and Laura began to contemplate his retirement from the ministry, and how they would enjoy their later years together.

He had been suffering from frequent bladder problems, and by 1874 his condition had worsened. Nevertheless, he and Laura traveled south to spend the winters with his daughter Helen, who was now a teacher in West Springfield, Massachusetts. During their visit, the Reverend took ill and decided to return home to recuperate and rest. On Friday, February 27, he and Laura headed back home to Winchendon. The following Monday, March 2, 1874, Brigham died suddenly in Winchendon.

He was remembered as "a man of earnest and consistent piety, of fair literary attainments, and had a life filled

173

with usefulness. He was always doing good things to all men as he had opportunity."[35]

The Reverend Willard Brigham was laid to rest in the Brigham family plot in the Riverside Cemetery in Winchendon, next to his first wife Maria. He would later be joined by his second wife and three of his four children.

---

[35] From the Williams College Obituary Record

REV. EDWARD FLINT BROOKS '38
"The 'Itinerant' Preacher"

Born: September 27, 1812
Died: September 15, 1872 (Age 59)
Buried: Channing Cemetery
                 Elgin, Illinois
Marriage: 1840s
                 Harriet E. (Brooks)
Children: Two
Occupation: Minister
Dorm Room: 1 West College

Edward F. Brooks is the only one of the Fraternity's
Founders to hail from the Green Mountain State of
Vermont. He was born September 27, 1812 in Halifax,
Vermont to Asa and Rebecca Brooks.

Nearing age twenty-two, Brooks enrolled at Williams,
like most of the freshmen, to begin the fall term in 1834.
He and his roommate, Charles Peabody, moved into
Room One on the second floor, where seventy percent of
the freshman Founders resided. Together, he and
Peabody would answer the call, both to joining the
Social Fraternity and choosing the ministry as their
profession.

Not one to establish firm roots in any one place, he
schooled at Williams only for two years before leaving
after the spring term in 1836 and transferring to
Washington College in Chestertown, Maryland, where
he graduated with a Bachelor of Arts degree in 1839.
Feeling the call to the ministry, he decided to continue
his studies at Princeton Theological Seminary in New
Jersey, where fellow Founder Lewis Lockwood was then

175

attending. Brooks would stay in touch with the Fraternity through his frequent correspondence and crossing of paths with Lockwood throughout their lives.

By the end of 1842, he was married to his sweetheart, Harriet, from Vermont. He had also been ordained as a Presbyterian minister in Raritan, New Jersey on October 20 of that year. He received his first ministerial call to French Creek, Virginia, where he stayed through 1843.

In 1844, he and Harriet moved to the eastern tip of Long Island, New York, to pastor a church in Riverhead, where coincidentally, Lewis Lockwood would eventually retire. It was during this two-year stint in Riverhead that Edward and Harriet would welcome Herbert G. Brooks, the first of their two children, in 1845.

The next year, Brooks received a new call to pastor a church in West Woodstock, Connecticut, so the Brooks and their infant son moved to the other side of Long Island Sound and into the northeast corner of Connecticut. In 1848, their second child, this time a daughter, Gertrude, was born. The young family stayed in Connecticut for two more years before moving again with the pastor's new call, back to New Jersey, to a pastorate in Manchester.

After barely a year in Manchester, and for the next twenty-one years, they would move time and again to various callings in Gill, Massachusetts, Mansfield and Westminster, Connecticut and Paris, New York.

By 1870, their two children were grown and out on their own. With the start of 1872, Reverend Brooks began feeling that his work in Paris, New York was done and contemplated yet another move. Deciding to step out of his comfort zone of New England, the fifty-nine year old and his wife made their longest move yet, and headed west to answer a pastoral call in Elgin, Illinois. This move would be his last.

The Presbyterian Church in Elgin had just finished building a new church structure, at the cost of more than $14,000 to accommodate their fast-growing congregation. Their current pastor, Reverend Donald Fletcher, was set to retire after the new church building's dedication on July 11, 1872. The reins of the church were then handed over to Reverend Brooks. The second half of 1872 would not be as celebratory as the first for the church, however. After less than two months in the pulpit, their new pastor Edward Brooks died suddenly just two weeks before his sixtieth birthday. Three months later in December 1872, their new church caught fire and burned to the ground.

The remainder of the Edward Brooks story is equally sad. After his death, Harriet laid him to rest at the Channing Street Cemetery in Elgin, before she presumably returned to Vermont. Channing Cemetery was the main cemetery in Elgin, until it reached capacity, and the City of Elgin opened Bluff City Cemetery in 1889. Burials at Channing Cemetery ceased right after the turn of the century and the cemetery began to fall into a state of disrepair. In the 1940s, officials decided to exhume the remains of those buried in Channing Cemetery and move them to Bluff City Cemetery. Those remains that were not claimed were either moved, or in some cases, "whatever remained of the remains" were simply bulldozed as

Elgin made way to use the land for the building of an elementary school, which still exists on the grounds today. Again, from the best records available, it appears that Brother Brooks' remains were not claimed or buried elsewhere. So, what was left of his remains was likely bulldozed into a mass grave, to a spot that is now forever hidden in the lush landscape behind the school building. The memory of Brother Brooks resides in beautiful parkland behind Channing Memorial Elementary School and in a solitary rock on the school's grounds that contains a plaque, dedicated to the memory of those who were once buried at Channing Cemetery.

HON. WILLIAM BROSS '38
"Father Bross"

Born:	November 4, 1813
Died:	January 27, 1890 (Age 76)
Buried:	Rosehill Cemetery
	Chicago, Illinois
Marriage:	October 7, 1839
	Mary J. Jansen (d. 5/25/1902)
Children:	Eight
Occupation:	Teacher, Businessman, Editor,
	Politician, Author
Dorm Room:	4 West College

The Honorable William Bross was one of the more
public of our Founders, and almost certainly the most
active in the Fraternity after his graduation. His
correspondence, convention attendance and his
continued interaction with Delta Upsilon and its
members, especially later in life, endeared him to
hundreds if not thousands of Delta Upsilon men in his
lifetime. His active participation, combined with his
"Founding Father" status, earned him the beloved
nickname, "Father Bross".

William Bross was one of two Founders who celebrated
their birthday with a fateful meeting in West College on
November Fourth, the other being Stephen Field.
William was born in an old log house on November 4,
1813 in Port Jervis, New York, and was the oldest of the
eleven children of Deacon Moses and Jane Bross. The
span of his siblings was twenty-three years, with the

179

William Bross
Williams 1838

youngest two brothers born after their older brother had founded the Fraternity!

Most of his childhood was spent back and forth between Port Jervis and a cabin in the woods that his parents had adopted as a summer residence in Milford, Pennsylvania; a whole seven miles away from Port Jervis. By the time he had reached his twentieth birthday, Bross has built himself up into an imposing brawn of a man by working at lumbering camps and lumber mills, and had saved enough money to put himself through college. In 1834, he headed to Williamstown and enrolled in Williams College. It was while at Williams in his first semester that he would come into contact with the likes of Stephen Field, who also lived in West College. Bross was the most outgoing of the new freshmen, the most universally liked and certainly, one of the brightest. Bross would also be strategically "hand-picked" to join the non-secret effort in the early going, which would certainly help to influence a great number of the freshman class to join the cause as well. Bross, living in Room Four in West College, roomed virtually in the center of the entire group of freshman in the dorm and would easily secure a good number of them to join the new Fraternity's cause, including his roommate, John H. Westfall.

While at Williams, he was an excellent and involved student. Besides his involvement in the Fraternity, he also served as President of the Philotechnian Society. His oratorical skills, learned at Williams, led to his being chosen as the Commencement Speaker at his graduation. After four years of study that was deep-rooted in classical literature, science and history, Bross graduated in 1838 with honors, including admission to

Phi Beta Kappa. He moved back to Pennsylvania to settle in Ridgebury, near his adopted home of Milford, to take a job at the Ridgebury Academy. There he would teach and serve as Principal for the next five years, with another five years following in a similar position in Chester, Pennsylvania. Upon his initial arrival in Ridgebury, however, he reacquainted with a young lady who had lived near him while growing up in Milford. On October 7, 1839, less than a year after graduating from college, William Bross married Miss Mary J. Jansen, the only daughter of Dr. John Jansen of Goshen, New York. Their marriage would produce eight children from 1840 to 1856, but sadly, only one of their children would live to adulthood, with the other seven dying as infants. Born September 27, 1844, their daughter and fourth child, Jessie, would be the apple of their eyes.

In 1846, Bross would make a trip to the Midwest that would alter his life forever. There he had an affair; not with a person, but with a city. While visiting the Midwest, he fell in love with Chicago and the city returned his affection. After returning to Pennsylvania from this trip, Bross made all of the necessary preparations, and within a little over a year, Bross and his wife and daughter had packed all of their belongings and headed west to settle in Chicago. By 1848, and now settled in Illinois, Bross changed his career and set out to enter the business of bookselling. He opened a store at 121 Lake Street in Chicago and ran it for about a year or so until about 1851, when he investigated a career in journalism and subsequently teamed up with the Rev. J. Ambrose Wight, a friend from Williams College. Together they took over production of *The Herald of the Prairies* newspaper. Bross and Wight produced the paper for about a year, after which Bross sold his interests to Wight and then formed a partnership with J.L. Scripps to begin producing the *Daily Democratic Press.* Bross and Scripps borrowed heavily for the high speed printing presses and other necessary equipment, which included the first copper faced type to be used in Illinois. The paper did well and served the people of Chicago, while going up against the other major papers; the *Daily Tribune* and the *Chicago Times.* The *Press* proved to be an excellent business and commercial publication and continued to improve and grow for the next couple of years. On July 1, 1858, after barely seven years in business, the *Daily Democratic Press* merged with the *Daily Tribune,* becoming the *Press-Tribune.* William Bross stayed on throughout the merger and became president and chief editor of the publication, and in 1860, they dropped the "Press" in the name and the paper became simply, the *Chicago Tribune.* Bross would stay with the *Tribune* for the remainder of his career.

While continuing to work hard to operate the *Tribune,* he also became very successful as a real estate investor, which helped him to gain substantial wealth. An avid supporter of Chicago, he was also keenly interested in Chicago's growth. In the 1850s, Bross was part of a consortium that purchased parcels of land about thirty miles north of Chicago, and helped to develop the area, which is still known today as Lake Forest. The parcels of land that they purchased were sold under very carefully restricted deeds, which helped to build an endowment fund that is now administered by Lake Forest College. The College, and the city of Lake Forest itself, were built out of the vision of William Bross and others. Lake Forest Academy and Ferry Hall Girls

Preparatory School were once part of the Lake Forest College development, as were the Rush Medical College and the Kent College of Law. These schools and the existing Lake Forest College today, stand as a fitting tribute to Bross.

While he was operating the *Press*, Bross began to take an interest in local politics, associating with the Republican Party. He ran for and won a seat on the Chicago City Council, where he served from 1855 to 1857. He would complete the merger of the *Press* and *Tribune* in 1858 and do right by the paper, by giving it his full attention for the next few years. These years were crucial for the paper itself, and for the country as it entered the Civil War.

Bross's appetite for politics, however, was still very acute. While serving on the City Council, and by virtue of his standing at the *Tribune*, he made the acquaintance of and became good friends with a soon to be even more popular lawyer in Springfield who had once served the state of Illinois in the U.S. House of Representatives. By the late 1850s, Abraham Lincoln had gained prominence, and Bross rallied behind his lawyer friend in support of Lincoln's next step, the United States Presidency. In fact, under Bross and his associates, the *Tribune* became the first newspaper in the country to publicly endorse Lincoln for the presidency. Bross campaigned for Lincoln and was with him at the 1860 Republican Convention in Chicago, Illinois that formally nominated Lincoln for President. Bross would support his friend throughout his presidency and further into Lincoln's re-election in 1864. Bross counted Lincoln among his most intimate friends and several times spoke from the same platform as Lincoln. By the end of the 1864 campaign, Bross himself was fully enamored with party politics.

In January 1865, Bross himself ran for and was successfully elected Lieutenant Governor of Illinois. Just three months later his friend, President Lincoln, would be dead from an assassin's bullet. It would be Bross' job to assist Illinois Governor Richard Oglesby in preparing the citizens of Illinois for the return of their native son for the various train stops, funeral corteges and burial. Bross's interest in politics would not last. Apparently four years in state government and the loss of his friend were enough to quench his appetite for politics. In 1869, after just one term as Lieutenant Governor, Bross said goodbye to public service and returned full-time to Chicago, and back to his more comfortable chair at the *Tribune*. However, upon his return, he took on more of a management role in reassuming the presidency of the paper, rather than the more detailed roles he had previously taken, which included editing and writing for the paper itself. He would continue as president of the paper until his last day.

On the evening of October 8, 1871, a fire broke out that spread through the city of Chicago over the next two days. Known as "The Great Chicago Fire", which incorrectly brought fame to Mrs. O'Leary's cow, the conflagration devastated the city that had been built largely of wood. Bross suffered immeasurable damage with the loss of his home and the offices at the *Tribune* virtually destroyed. Bross, however, directed an issue to be printed from a makeshift press, which hit the streets after the fire had burned out. While most people would lament their loss, the fire seemed to energize Bross.

Already, he had a reputation for being strong and energetic in all that he undertook, as well as possessing a good work ethic and endurance. He always professed an enthusiastic affinity for Chicago, and the fire only spurred him into action to help his beloved adopted city rebound.

Bross's selfless ambition and positive outlook took him to New York City immediately after the fire, to make a plea. He saw the fire as an opportunity to make Chicago bigger and better than it ever had been, and he would be right. While in New York, he would virtually preach to anyone and everyone in New York, urging them to travel to Chicago, not only to help, but to set up residence. A major city in need of severe rebuilding held much opportunity for tradesmen and for nearly every area of commercial business. There was money to be made and prosperity to be had as a result of the fire, and while a good many people did indeed prosper as a result of the rebuilding process, the true winner was the city itself. Bross's optimism proved prophetic, and Chicago came back stronger than ever. Bross himself would rebuild and settle into a home at 194 Michigan Avenue.

For the next several years, Bross traveled extensively, writing articles about his travels for the *Tribune* and campaigning for other Republican would-be office seekers. In 1875 though, he would accept his most cherished role yet. He would become...a grandfather. His daughter, Jessie, had met and married Henry Demarest Lloyd, whom Bross hired as a journalist at the *Tribune* in 1872. Lloyd, the notable muckraker who would eventually be hailed in his later years as the "Father of Investigative Journalism," caught the eye of

William Bross
Williams 1838

the boss's daughter and married her a year later on Christmas Day 1873. On February 24, 1875, Jessie Bross Lloyd gave birth to Bross's namesake, William Bross Lloyd. Bross doted solely on his young grandson until a second grandson, Demarest Lloyd, was born in 1882. Years later, William Bross Lloyd himself would become a millionaire journalist and socialist like his father, and eventually, a co-founder of the Communist Labor Party.

In about 1880, Brother Bross began to suffer from a kidney illness. And while he continued working and holding an office at the *Tribune*, he slowed his work a bit to take on only special projects that he had a strong desire to tackle in his semi-retirement. Much of his time was spent in the vision and further development of Lake Forest College. During this time he also gifted several thousands of dollars to the institution. Toward the end of his life, he would also continue to serve as Chairman of the Board of Trustees of the College. A visit to his office would often see various plans and blueprints spread about the room, showing the next developmental plan for the College, or the continued advancement of Chicago itself. He wrote a number of books, which included A History of Camp Douglas and History of Chicago, in addition to a compilation of all of his editorials from the *Tribune*. He continued to hold a great interest in the goings-on of the Fraternity as well.

In 1884, he was invited to chair the business meetings and serve as Honorary President of the Fiftieth Convention of Delta Upsilon, which he accepted. The following excerpt from the *Delta Upsilon Quarterly* in January 1885 recaps the Convention and the high esteem that the membership had for "Father Bross":

The Fiftieth Annual Convention of the Delta Upsilon
Fraternity was held with the New York Chapter on the
fourth and fifth of December in 1884. The business
sessions were presided over by ex-Governor Bross. The
Banquet to the Semi-centennial Convention was held at
Delmonico's on the evening of December 5, 1884. Ex-
Governor Bross was the first speaker at the banquet, and
as he rose, a perfect thunder of applause greeted him.
Most in attendance wished that more of the Founding
Fathers could have been there to witness this, and stated
that Mr. Bross had to take more applause than one man
could well respond to. In his talk, he told about the early
struggles of the Fraternity in Williams College, how he
had watched its progress for fifty years, and how he
approved of what it is now doing. He hoped that it
would extend its benefits to colleges over the whole
country and restrict itself to no section. Bross, who was
also affectionately addressed as "Father" Bross because
of his status as a Founding Father of the Fraternity, was
surrounded during the intervals between the sessions of
business by an enthusiastic gathering anxious to make
his acquaintance and secure his autograph.

Among the letters that were received at the *Delta
Upsilon Quarterly* office in New York both before and
after that convention, none was more interesting to the
members of the Fraternity than the following letter on
Tribune letterhead received from Bross after his
attendance at the Fiftieth Convention. The following
letter was sent to Frederick Crossett, then Business
Manager of the *Delta Upsilon Quarterly* magazine and a
member of the Fraternity's Board of Directors:

The Tribune.

Chicago, Dec 16th 1884

Mr. Fred M. Crossett

My Dear Sir

Permit me to express to you the great pleasure I enjoyed at the semi centennial celebration of the D. U. Fraternity in New York, Dec 9th & 10th. While with Kirke White "I sighed that I was all alone" there, of all those who formed the society in the fall of 1834 — fifty years ago — I could and did most heartily rejoice that what began in Williams College amid jeers and sneers, ridicule and rebuffs of all kinds had spread into

Image courtesy of Williams College
Archives and Special Collections

190

The Tribune.

Chicago, Dec. 16, 1884
Mr. Fred M. Crossett,

My Dear Sir:

Permit me to express to you the great pleasure I enjoyed at the Semi-centennial celebration of the Delta Upsilon Fraternity in New York, December 4th and 5th. While with Kirk White "I sighed that I was all alone" there of those who formed the society in the fall of 1834 – fifty years ago. I could and did most heartily rejoice that what began in Williams College amid jeers and sneers, ridicule and rebuffs of all kinds, had spread into

so many leading colleges
and had become
almost national in the
power and beneficent
influence it exerts
in moulding the character
of those who are sent
its minister at, and
in fact largely control
the very sources of
public opinion. Then
my conviction is clear
and decided that
our Society has influence
direct and powerful
to make men of more
generous and broader
views than its more
narrow and secret
competitors in the four
years of college life.
Such was my estimate
of the men assembled
at our semicentennial;

so many leading colleges, and had become almost national in power and beneficent influence it exerts in moulding the character of those who are soon to minister at, and, in fact, largely control the very sources of public opinion. For my conviction is clear and decided that our society has a direct and powerful influence to make men of more generous and broader views than its more narrow and secret competitors in the four years of college life. Such was my estimate of the men assembled at our Semi-centennial,

and such I think is
warranted by the
past history of the mem-
bers of our Society. The
honored name of Pres-
ident Garfield will
at once become as an
illustration of this
fact. I trust that you
and many others of
those present, will honor
by your presence, the
Centennial of the Society,
and impress upon its
members all the best
principles of our Christian
civilization. Please
present to them the best
wishes of one, I think
I may safely say, of all
its founders. God bless
and even prosper our
noble Society.

Very truly
Fraternally yours _____ Williams '38

Image courtesy of Williams College
Archives and Special Collections

and such, I think, is warranted by the past history of the members of our society. The honored name of President Garfield will at once occur as an illustration of this fact. I trust that you and many others of those present will honor by your presence the centennial of the society, and impress upon its members all the best principles of our Christian civilization. Please present to them the best wishes of one – I think I might safely say of all its founders. God Bless and ever prosper our noble society.

Very truly and fraternally yours,

Wm. Bross
Williams, '38

In his later years, Bross remained active but tried his best to remain in semi-retirement. He readily accepted visitors at his home, and lived the life of a "benevolent and well-loved Chicago squire". In May of 1888, however, he suffered a severe stroke while attending to his editorial duties at the *Tribune* offices. The stroke partially paralyzed him and nearly proved fatal. He was moved to the home of his daughter in Winnetka, Illinois, where he received treatment from the most skilled doctors in Chicago, while receiving comfort from the caring hands of his family. Everything that could be done for him was done. After about four weeks of recuperating, Bross began to show signs of progress and family and friends felt hopeful of his recovery as he slowly moved out of danger. While he continued to make progress, he was never fully the same. The once energetic and vibrant Bross was beginning to show the years of hard-driving determination and hard work.

Bross would carry on for a little more than another year and a half before he quietly slipped away. Ironically, he died not from the effects of the stroke, but from the kidney disease that had plagued him for ten years. His funeral was held at the Second Presbyterian Church in Chicago, where he was a faithful member and steadfast supporter. He was laid to rest in Chicago's Rosehill Cemetery, where many prominent Chicagoans are interred. The impressive monument that marks his final resting place to this day stands as a fitting memorial to a dedicated DU and Chicago leader.

REV. THOMAS AMORY HALL '38
"The Chaplain"

Born: September 2, 1813
Died: September 17, 1871 (Age 58)
Buried: Otis Cemetery
                 Otis, Massachusetts
Marriage: August 25, 1840
                 Mary Strong (d. 3/22/1889)
Children: One
Occupation: Teacher, Minister
Dorm Room: ? West College[36]

Thomas Amory Hall was one of three freshmen
Founders born in Hawley, Massachusetts and the
youngest of the three, born on September 2, 1813. He
was a very bright individual, and was one of only four of
the thirty to have been a Phi Beta Kappa member.[37] He
and Theophilus Page, also from Hawley, enrolled at
Williams in the fall of 1834 and likewise, joined the
Social Fraternity meeting in November. While at
Williams, Hall was a dutiful student. He was President
of the Philologian Society and rose near the top of his
class, graduating as the Salutatorian for the Class of
1838.

For the three years immediately following his
graduation from Williams, he taught classes and was
Principal at the Mountain Seminary in Worthington,
Massachusetts. At the same time he studied theology

---

[36] It is not known which room Hall occupied in 1834, due to his transferring in
after the directory was printed. Most likely, he shared an available room on the
fourth floor, as the second and third floors were full, according to the directory.
[37] The other Founders in Phi Beta Kappa were Bross, Field and Pise.
Pise was honorary.

under the private tutelage of Reverend John H. Bisbee. Like many Founders before him, he waited until his studies were complete before getting married. On August 25, 1840 he married Miss Mary Strong, three years his senior, in Southampton, Massachusetts. In December of that same year, he was licensed to preach by what was then the "Old Hampshire Association" at Southampton. On June 18, 1841, he was ordained and installed as the new pastor of the Congregational Church in Dalton, Massachusetts. It was in Dalton, less than a year later on May 6, 1842, that Hall's wife gave birth to their only child, their daughter, Mary.

He pastored in Dalton until 1847 when he moved down the road, south of town, to take charge of the Academy in Lee, Massachusetts, where he also taught classes. He remained there for eight years until his health began to slip. He then returned to the pulpit in 1856 at the Congregational Church in Otis, Massachusetts, where he would remain for another eight years, earning a salary of five-hundred dollars per year.

In August of 1864, the fifty-one year old minister began serving a short stint in the Civil War as Chaplain of the Twenty-Fifth Regiment of the United States Colored Troops. He joined that command in Jacksonville, Florida in October, and then served for much of the time in Charleston, South Carolina. Hall ministered in this capacity until his discharge from the Army on June 7, 1865. Following the completion of his Army service, he immediately returned to Massachusetts and answered a call to preach at the church in Monterey, Massachusetts, where he stayed for six years.

On September 17, 1871, just two weeks after turning fifty-eight years old, Reverend Thomas A. Hall passed away, bringing an end to a good and useful life. He was buried on the side of the hill at the Otis Cemetery, in direct view of the church where he served as a good and faithful preacher.

REV. JOHN PEABODY HILLS '38
"The Mysterious One"

Born: January 29, 1810
Died: 1856
Buried: Unknown
Marriage: Cynthia Kimball
Children: Three
Occupation: Minister
Dorm Room: 2 – West College

John Peabody Hills is yet another Founder for whom little information exists, and one of two whose final whereabouts remain a mystery.

Hills was born just across the Massachusetts border from Williamstown in Hancock, New Hampshire on January 29, 1810. He entered Williams with his class, settling in Room Two near the rest of the "freshmen seven" on the second floor. John schooled at Williams for only two years before leaving after the spring term in 1836. He transferred to Ohio and enrolled at Marietta College where he graduated with a Bachelor of Arts degree in 1839.

He fell in love with and married Cynthia Kimball of Kennebunk, Maine. After they married, they moved to Cincinnati, Ohio where in 1840, John enrolled at Lane Theological Seminary. A year later, he was joined there by Lewis Lockwood, who arrived for his final year of seminary. While in seminary, Cynthia gave birth to the couple's first child, with her namesake, Cynthia, arriving in 1841.

Shortly after graduating from seminary, John answered a call to pastor a church in Adams, Ohio. Barely getting settled in Adams, Cynthia and John welcomed their second daughter, Delia, in 1842. John pastored in Adams for the next eight years and would welcome their third daughter, Alice, in 1848. Shortly after Alice's arrival, the family moved west to answer a call in Illinois. They settled in Edgar County, Illinois by 1850, with John pastoring in churches in Manchester and Oakford, Illinois.

Little else is known of the Reverend John P. Hills or his family. John died sometime in 1856, presumably in Illinois. His burial and the whereabouts of his family are unknown except for daughter, Delia. Delia never married, but found jobs as a housemaid or nanny, with stops for several years at a time in Colorado, New Mexico and finally, by 1920, in California.

Everything else...is a mystery.

REV. FOSTER LILLY '38
"Pride of the Presbytery"

Born:	June 6, 1812
Died:	December 23, 1855 (Age 43)
Buried:	Unknown
Marriage:	1847
	Caroline Bentley
Children:	One
Occupation:	Minister
Dorm Room:	3 West College

It is ironic that the two Founders for whom their final whereabouts are unknown are side-by-side, both alphabetically within their class, and in rooming assignments in West College...

Foster Lilly was the tenth of the fourteen children of Foster and Deborah Lilly. The Lilly Family originally hailed from Ashfield, Massachusetts but then moved to Hawley and Buckland before settling in an area in Broome County, New York, known as Castle Creek. It was while living in Hawley that Foster, the sixth of their seven sons, was born on June 6, 1812, less than two weeks before the United States went to war with Great Britain in the War of 1812.

When young Foster enrolled at Williams, he actually "hailed" from Chenango, New York. However, he was still one of three Founders, along with Thomas Hall and Theophilus Page, born in Hawley, Massachusetts. Foster's eldest brother, Alvah, had attended Williams before him, graduating with the class of 1824, so it seemed natural for Foster to follow. He would also have a legacy follow him into the Fraternity when his

203

younger brother, Aruna, would enroll at Williams and also join the Social Fraternity, graduating in 1848.

Foster and his roommate Francis Williams were among the "second floor freshmen," and joined together. Lilly and Francis Williams were a natural match, as Williams hailed from Ashfield, where Lilly's family had originally lived. After graduating from Williams College in 1838, Foster joined Ephraim Kellogg and Josiah Lyman at Auburn Theological Seminary. He studied there and became licensed to preach on April 15, 1840 by the Presbytery of Tioga County, New York. After graduating from the seminary, he immediately accepted a pastorate in Chenango Forks, New York near the family home, and for a short time in Ontario, Canada.

One year later, Lilly took a pastorate further south in Broome County, in the new settlement of Deposit, New York. He pastored there for three years before spending another four in Hornellsville, in the western part of the state. In 1847, he married Caroline Bentley from Broome County, New York. On February 18, 1848, their only child, Willy, was born. On September 11, 1849, Lilly would be fully ordained as a Presbyterian minister in Spencer, New York. He would spend the rest of his short life ministering and doing mission work in the central part of New York, spending time in Spencer, Kennedyville, Wheeler and Hume. In 1852, at the age of four, young Willy Lilly died. Three years later, just two days before Christmas in 1855, Willy's father, the Reverend Foster Lilly also slipped away from his earthly labor at the age of forty-two, in Andover, New York.

There is a Lilly Family Cemetery in a rural part of Castle Creek, New York near the former Lilly family homestead. Some of Lilly's siblings, and the remains of his parents, Foster Sr. and Deborah, rest in the cemetery. However, records do not show that this is the final resting place of Foster Lilly, the Founder. He may simply be buried in an unmarked grave in the Lilly Cemetery, or someplace between Castle Creek and Andover, where he died. Regardless, Foster Lilly's final resting place is currently unknown.

THEOPHILUS PAGE '38
"The Silent Man"

Born:	July 4, 1813
Died:	January 3, 1895 (Age 81)
Buried:	Rahway Cemetery
	Rahway, New Jersey
Marriage:	None
Children:	None
Occupation:	Teacher, News-dealer, Merchant
Dorm Room:	14 West College

At a time when most citizens of the United States were
enjoying picnics and other July Fourth celebrations in
town squares all across the nation, Mrs. Page had other
responsibilities. It wasn't that she was anti-social; it
was simply that her time had come. For in the tiny
little hamlet of Hawley, Massachusetts, Mrs. Page was
at home, unable to participate in the festivities to
celebrate the thirty-seventh anniversary of the birth of a
nation. She was in labor, preparing for another type of
birth. On July 4, 1813, she brought a baby boy into the
world. Mrs. Page named her son Theophilus.

Theophilus Page is arguably one of the more intriguing
members of the elite club of Founding Fathers. He was
raised and schooled in Hawley, and lived there until it
was time for him to go to college. He settled on
Williams College and joined the class of 1838. He lived
on the third floor of West College among several other
Founders of the Fraternity. He roomed with Cole Denio
of South Shaftsbury, Vermont, just across the border
from Williams. While Denio did not join the effort of the
Social Fraternity at its birth, he was influenced
afterward by Page, who had a clear and dedicated

interest in the Fraternity. Cole Denio became one of the first to be recruited in the days following the Social Fraternity's birth.

After his graduation from Williams, he taught school for two years before seeking a career change to the world of business. In 1840, he moved to 38 Main Street in Rahway, New Jersey, and for the next several years of his life, he sold newspapers. He was not the likely street corner salesman, but rather a specialist who maintained and sold a stock of various publications. By all accounts, he was primarily a news merchant, supplying the local citizens with knowledge of current events from all over the world. Day after day, in winter and summer, he supplied his customers. Throughout his many years in this venture, he sold the first editions of most of the New York newspapers.

Whether it was during his time in college, or shortly thereafter is not exactly known, but somewhere between the years of 1838 and 1844, Theophilus began to withdraw himself socially. His life took on a sense of mystery, which no one was able to solve. Even those who knew him were largely unable to crack what appeared to be a tough social exterior and get to know him personally. The generally accepted theory was that it was a case of unrequited love that caused him to become a recluse. Whatever the reason, Page virtually limited himself to a simple "yes" or "no" in conversation. It was very peculiar, especially given the fact that for nearly fifty years he would be in daily contact with the public. Nevertheless, Page earned his reputation and likewise the nickname, "The Silent Man'.

This excerpt that appeared in both the *Delta Upsilon Quarterly* and the <u>Williams College Obituary Record</u> gives some insight into the man and his life:

"Up to 1876 he was strong and healthy, but one morning in that year while he was waiting at the railroad for his papers, a mail bag, thrown from a fast train, struck him, and his right thigh was broken in two places. This was the only serious break in his business, and he was laid up for several months. He received $5,000 by the railroad company as a settlement. Since the time of the accident, he always went about on crutches."

"He is thought to have been wealthy, but always rented a single room and lived alone. In one instance he is known to have dunned[38] a man for twenty years before obtaining pay for some papers he had delivered. No one ever saw him angry, and he never uttered a curse (word) that is remembered."[39]

"He was a regular attendant at church, being a Presbyterian.[40] When the great bell of the church was purchased he gave $500 toward it. This surprised everyone, as he had the reputation of being a miser. He was led to the large gift through a wealthy man remarking he would "give as much as Page." Page smiled, one of the few times he is known to have done so, and subscribed $500 and paid the money down."

"He was of an ingenious turn of mind and worked on a number of inventions, several of which are said to be

---

[38] Dunned *v.t.* - to make persistent demands upon, esp. for payment of a debt."
[39] From the <u>Williams College Obituary Record</u>
[40] In fact, he was a founding member of the Second Presbyterian Church in Rahway, New Jersey, which still exists today.

practicable. When he became ill some time ago he rigged up an apparatus to turn himself in bed, he not having the strength to do so. He had simply to pull a rope with one hand. His room was strikingly similar to the description of a room given by Dickens in his 'Old Curiosity Shop.' In a corner was a wagon designed by Mr. Page as a self-propeller. Scattered around were curios of all descriptions."

In 1886, after forty-six years in business, and at the age of seventy-three, Page decided to retire. His later years were spent in relative seclusion, left to his own thoughts, but still regularly attending church every Sunday. On January 3, 1895, "The Silent Man" silently and peacefully passed away in his home, filled with his creative ideas.

Although his tombstone over his grave denotes incorrect dates for his birth, the monument itself stands strong in a full plot of its own in a back section of the Rahway Cemetery. It is an impressive yet ironic memorial to one who was so silent and reserved throughout his life.

The final words, quoted from the same obituary earlier, could indeed stand as a fitting epitaph:

"He earned for himself in the last fifty years of his life one of the noblest of human titles, 'The Silent Man'. His memory should be honored by all that appreciate the importance of silence. Theophilus Page was a silent reproach to the eternal, inconsequential babbling of this age."

REV. CHARLES PEABODY '38
"Mr. New England"

Born:	July 1, 1810
Died:	February 9, 1896 (Age 85)
Buried:	Springfield Cemetery Springfield, Massachusetts
Marriage:	Almira (Porter) White November 13, 1841 (d. 1856)
Marriage:	December 10, 1857 Emily S. Ball
Children:	One
Occupation:	Minister
Dorm Room:	1 West College

Charles Peabody was the second of nine children of John and Elizabeth (Lucy) Peabody, born in Peterborough, New Hampshire on July 1, 1810. At the age of twenty-one, and during a time when religious revival was beginning in full force, Charles traveled south to Chicopee, Massachusetts, near Springfield, to attend a religious conference. It was there that he made the decision to seek the ministry as his chosen profession, like many other men in this time period.

In the fall of 1834, Charles enrolled at Williams, which by that time had already established a fine reputation of preparing students for a career in the ministry. Williams was also the natural choice given its close proximity to Peterborough and his family. He roomed with Edward Brooks in Room One, and like so many other freshmen, on the second floor.
After his graduation in 1838, Peabody and fellow Fraternity brother, Willard Brigham, set out for Andover Theological Seminary, the oldest graduate

school of theology in the United States, founded primarily by Calvinists after a growing split within the Congregational Churches. This and other factors, essentially, helped spark a religious revival and a need for many additional ministers.

Peabody went back to Williamstown after graduating from Andover in 1841, to marry his sweetheart whom he had met while at Williams. Almena Porter was six years his senior. Charles and Almena were married on November 15, 1841, and Charles was ordained at Biddeford, Maine three weeks later on December eighth. He set out on his "ministerial tour" of New England, and after the first of the New Year in 1842; he assumed the role of pastor at a church in Barrington, Rhode Island.

After four years in Rhode Island, they moved to Ashford, Connecticut for another four years. In 1850, they moved again, back to the area around Williams College, to pastor in Windsor, Massachusetts and Pownal, Vermont. While in Pownal, Charles and Almena's nearly fourteen-year marriage would come to an abrupt end, with Almena's death in September of 1856.

Within a couple of months of Almena's death, the now forty-six year old Charles met and began a courtship with the thirty-nine year old Emily Sophia Ball of Lee, Massachusetts. In April of 1857, Charles was invited to return to the place of his ordination, to pastor a church in Biddeford, Maine. Emily would soon follow him there, and the two would be married on December 10, 1857. Together Emily and Charles would have their only child, a son, Clarence, and for the next ten years, would live as a family in Maine. In 1867, the Peabody's would begin making the trek gradually back west, with pastoral stops in Eliot, Maine and Epsom, New Hampshire, concluding in 1875 in Ashburnham, Massachusetts. It was the stop in Epsom, New Hampshire that completed the tour, with Peabody having held pastoral duties in each of the six New England states.

In 1875, now age sixty-five and in a period of ill health, he decided to retire from full-time ministry and go back to the place he loved the most, and to where his passion for life as a minister began, near Chicopee. He and his family settled in Longmeadow, Massachusetts near Springfield, where he would remain for the rest of his life. The pastor regained his health and, for the next fifteen years, continued to preach as a guest pastor and conduct ministerial duties on an interim or supply basis. This description of him, from the *Delta Upsilon Quarterly* and Williams College annals provides the best testament to his character and personality:

"Mr. Peabody was one of the old school ministers. He was of commanding figure and had a finely expressive face. There was upon occasion a merry twinkle in his eye and he was of an affable and kindly disposition. Since his retirement to Longmeadow, he has in no way been conspicuous, but has enjoyed a hale old age, sedulously attended church meetings and ministerial and religious conferences of all sorts in this vicinity."

At the beginning of the New Year in January of 1890, the Reverend Charles Peabody, now eighty years old, hung up his clerical collar for good and retired from active and part-time ministry. He was now determined to simply enjoy his golden years with his wife by his side. Both of them enjoying good health, they celebrated their thirty-eighth wedding anniversary in December of 1895.

On February 8, 1896, Charles was up and around the house as usual. Still able and spry despite his eighty-five years, he was still in full command of his mental faculties. But, early the next morning his time came, and the Reverend Peabody quietly passed away in his sleep of ailments incident to old age. Three years later, Emily would be laid to rest beside him in the Springfield Cemetery.

REV. DR. DAVID PISE '38
"The Professor"

Born:	September 29, 1815
Died:	August 19, 1894 (Age 78)
Buried:	Spring Grove Cemetery
	Cincinnati, Ohio
Marriage:	June 24, 1846
	Amelia S. Allison (d. 1877)
Children:	Six
Occupation:	Minister
Dorm Room:	18 East College

In 1915, the steeple of Christ Church in Glendale, Ohio, was replaced, as were all but one of the bells that chime on Sundays and for various events. All of the bells were given names, just like "Big Ben" in England and others, because bells seemingly take on a personality of their own when they ring. One of the bells in the new steeple was dubbed, "Great David", named after the fourth rector and one of the most effective and beloved pastors of the church, the Reverend David Pise. Although the steeple was installed some twenty years after Pise's death, it showed just how revered he was to the Episcopal parish and how deep his character resonated with the people of Glendale.

David Pise was born September 29, 1815 in Belchertown, Massachusetts, just north of Springfield, near Northhampton. His long American lineage can be traced back to 1634 when his ancestors arrived from England. Somewhere along the way, his family

David Pise
Williams 1838

216

"Americanized" the surname, changing it to "Pease". Once David reached adulthood, sometime during or immediately after his days at Williams, he dug into old records and discovered the original spelling of his ancestral name and decided to change his name legally back to Pise to be more correct with his family history, which accounts for his name appearing one way or the other in different places. During the Revolutionary War, his grandfather was in charge of the military hospital on Block Island, thirteen miles south of Rhode Island in the Atlantic Ocean. His father was a Baptist clergyman until his death at age ninety-six. David's strong family history destined him to greatness as well.

Pise enrolled at Williams College in the fall of 1832 with the class of 1836, which would have made him a part of the junior class at the time of the Founding. He took extra time in his studies, however, which resulted in his graduation with the class of 1838. His roommate was Zalmon Richards, with whom he would maintain a cordial friendship throughout his lifetime. The two would join the Social Fraternity together. Even though he was enrolled continuously for six years, David either simply stretched his education out over a longer period of time, or more likely, stayed for additional study given his propensity for scholarship and academia.

While in college, Pise took a brief vacation visit to nearby Troy, New York. While there, although he was associated with the Baptist church, he attended an Episcopal church for the first time. He was struck by the tradition and beauty of the service and became instantly enamored. He began to study the history and doctrine of the Episcopal Church, and then went on to teach at the academies at Woodstock and Fayetteville,

217

New York. It was while he was in Fayetteville that he made the decision to withdraw from his Baptist affiliation and make the move to the Episcopal Church, not only as a member, but as a priest as well.

Despite his father's objections, he moved to New York City and began studying at the General Theological Seminary, which is today the oldest Episcopal seminary in the United States. He studied there for only one year before he was called away to teach again, becoming the private tutor for the family of James K. Marshall, the son of then recently deceased Chief Justice of the United States, John Marshall.

During his free time, he would continue his studies for the ministry, which led to his ordination on April 24, 1845. He was sent then, by deacon's orders, to the Christ Church in Manilus, New York, where he became its rector. The following year, on June 24, 1846, Pise married Amelia Southart Allison, a New York debutante. He led the church at Manilus for another three years, followed by a two-year return to Fayetteville, New York, where he was called to the Trinity Church. At the same time, he was re-elected principal of the Academy in Fayetteville, a position he had once held right after his graduation from Williams. One of his pupils at the Fayetteville Academy was a young boy named Stephen, the son of Richard Cleveland, the Presbyterian Minister in the village. Stephen proved to be a bright boy and a diligent student. Pise took great interest in the boy, as he did in all of his students, and helped to challenge Stephen to do his very best. Perhaps Pise's influence was at least part of the reason that Stephen would go on to a successful career in public service and leadership, first as a sheriff, and then on to Mayor of Buffalo, New York, and then as the Governor of New York state. In 1884, nearly forty years after Pise nurtured him as a student, the teacher would see his former student, Stephen "Grover" Cleveland become the twenty-second President of the United States.

In 1850, chronic bronchitis dictated a change of venue, and Pise and his wife moved south to Clarksville, Tennessee to accept a call from the Trinity Church there. During his fourteen years as rector in Tennessee, (four at Trinity Church, followed by ten at St. Peter's in Columbia, Tennessee), Pise earned a reputation as a formidable servant as well as a great power within the diocese. While in Tennessee, he was awarded the degree of Doctor of Divinity as well as an honorary Phi Beta Kappa designation from Stewart College, which is today known as Union University. He was also a founder of Sewanee: The University of the South, in Sewanee, Tennessee. He was offered the position of its President, which he declined for an unknown reason. He was also a candidate for Episcopal Bishop of Tennessee, which he would have most certainly been awarded had he not discouraged his own candidacy. As a "Yankee" in the south during the time of the Civil War, but one who believed in secession and states' rights, he would have almost certainly been confirmed. However, Pise's heart was not in the appointment because he did not like the daily details of being a Bishop, not the least of which was fundraising. Pise simply preferred to focus on his congregational work and being a shepherd of the people.

During this time in Tennessee, David and Amelia would welcome six children into their family: William,

Josephine, Francis, Charles, Elizabeth and Frederick. Although all of their children lived into adulthood, three of David's children would predecease him. His son, William T. Pise would follow in his father's footsteps and become a respected rector himself before succumbing to tuberculosis in 1882.

After several happy years in Tennessee, David preached for six years at St. Paul's Church in New Albany, Indiana, followed by a brief stint at St. Paul's Church in Portland, Maine, before his wife's fragile health forced a move back to the Midwest, closer to family. They settled in Glendale, Ohio in 1875. Pise took charge of the Christ Church in Glendale and moved into the rectory with his large family. Just two short years later, however, he was stricken with grief with the death of his beloved wife of thirty-one years. Despite his grief, he found comfort in his children and his congregation. His dependency on the Lord's work, however, would become more and more important with the additional loss of three of his children between 1880 and 1882. Pise, through his grief, maintained his focus and hectic schedule and continued to busy himself in the matters and business of the church.

In 1886, Reverend Pise, now age seventy, began to show his age. By November, his illness prevented him from taking part in Sunday services. By December, he began to recognize that a prolonged rest was in order so he decided to take a vacation with his oldest daughter, Josephine. "Josie" had taken over hostess and motherly duties after the death of her mother, and took great care of her father. Together he and Josie traveled to California, visiting several cities over the first three months of 1887 but still spending every Sunday in a parish either preaching or participating in the service somehow. Throughout this rest period, he remained dedicated to his calling and had no intent of resting in his service to God. By early April, he was back in Glendale, presiding over Palm Sunday services. The rest seemed to have certainly recharged him, but his youthful age and exuberance was definitely in his personal history by now. For the next couple of years, he continued about his daily activities, albeit a bit slower than he used to be. By the end of 1889, while he kept going, it was clear that he was far from well.

On September 29, 1890, Pise celebrated his seventy-fifth birthday. His church was on the move and they made plans for the addition of a Memorial Parish House in memory of Pise's eldest son, Rev. William T. Pise, who had died in 1882. So yet again, when Brother Pise seemed to be slowing down, he received a jolt of energy and was rejuvenated thanks to church progress. In addition, his daughter, Elizabeth (Lily), married, and his son, Charles, was called as rector to a church in Georgia. Many good things were happening, and Pise simply did not have time to slow down. Once again, he fought his own thoughts of retirement. In 1893, a severe nosebleed forced yet another vacation for Dr. Pise, this time a two-month sabbatical to Daytona, Florida. However, just as before, he was still participating in Sunday services, even performing the entire service in a church on Easter Sunday.

The week after Easter 1893, he was back in Glendale, as hard at work as ever in the life of Christ Church, which had grown, strengthened and become even more beautiful under his direction and leadership. In October 1893, he traveled back to Williamstown, Massachusetts for the one-hundredth anniversary celebration of Williams College. (No doubt the visit prompted a remembrance of his fraternal efforts nearly sixty years before.) On his way home from the college reunion, however, Pise was not well. Still, his determined spirit was unrelenting, and he kept going, even recuperating to the point of resuming his schedule and taking on an even heavier load than before.

For the next several months Pise would continue in his earthly labor. In August of 1894, it is documented that Pise performed the Sunday services unassisted on both the fifth and the twelfth of August. On Tuesday the fourteenth, Pise was ill again and in bed. This time, however, the familiar Pise rebound did not come. Fittingly, in the early morning of Sunday, August nineteenth, before the sun had even peeked over the horizon, David Pise finally received his due rest.

Pise was well loved by all who knew him especially within the Glendale community. He was described as being "in the largest and best sense 'a Father of God' to all his people." He was laid to rest in the Pise family plot in Spring Grove Cemetery in Cincinnati, next to his beloved wife and his three children, who preceded him in death.

"Great David" still rings in the bell tower at Christ Church in Glendale, Ohio today. David Pise's spirit still lives in each ring...a fitting memorial to a man who helped usher a church and a Fraternity into its own.

*The bell tower at Christ Church in Glendale,
Ohio where "Great David" resides to this day.*

Francis Williams
Williams 1838

REV. FRANCIS WILLIAMS '38
"The Orator"

Born: January 2, 1814
Died: January 8, 1896 (Age 82)
Buried: Chaplin Cemetery
               Chaplin, Connecticut
Marriage: September 22, 1841
               Mahala R. Badger
Children: Three
Occupation: Minister, Politician
Dorm Room: 3 West College

Francis Williams, like many of the other Founders, was
from a large family. He was born on January 2, 1814,
the fourth child of nine brothers and two sisters. He
was born and raised in Ashfield, Massachusetts, a city
which had been partially established by his grandfather,
Ephraim Williams, although not the same Ephraim
Williams who was the benefactor of Williams College.
Francis's younger brother Fordyce, who was fourteen
years his junior, would follow Francis into the
Fraternity, although not via Williams College. Fordyce
would not only join Delta Upsilon, but became a
founding member of the Rochester Chapter in 1852.

His father, Captain Israel Williams, was a soldier in the
War of 1812 and joined the great westward pioneer
movement in the early 1800s. In 1834, as Francis was
preparing to enter Williams College, Captain Williams
began preparing to move permanently west to an area
at the southern edge of Lake Geneva, Wisconsin, near
the Illinois-Wisconsin border, and built a house for his
family among the many Indian lodges that still
blanketed the area. He would become one of the first

justices in the area, and later, the village of Williams Bay, Wisconsin was named in his honor.

Growing up in Ashfield, Massachusetts would prepare Francis well for college there, like Lebbeus Phillips before him, at the Sanderson Academy, in addition to time at the Amherst Academy and at the academy in Shelburne Falls. He was active in church, even at a young age, becoming a member at the church in nearby Buckland. This experience helped forge his early decision to become a minister. In 1834, instead of following his father and family to Wisconsin, Francis enrolled at Williams College to begin the fall term. He settled nicely into Room Three of West College with his roommate, Foster Lilly, a friend who hailed from Hawley, Massachusetts, nine miles down the road from his hometown.

He was very active at Williams and enjoyed it immensely. He was a good and diligent student, and his hard work paid off with the honor of giving an oration at his college class commencement. He was one of the Moonlight Prize[41] speakers in his junior year, and was also President of the Philotechnian Society. He was also very active in the Social Fraternity, having been elected to and serving as the chapter president in his senior year.

Upon graduating from Williams, Francis, already having chosen the same profession as most of his fraternity brothers, entered into the field of ministry.

---

[41] Juniors and Sophomores competed in an oratorical contest the day before commencement. The winner of the contest was announced the next day. The name "Moonlight Prize" came from the fact that the contest was held in the evening after dark.

He headed to Connecticut, where he would essentially begin his love affair with that state. Joining five other fraternity brothers who graduated before him, he enrolled at the Hartford Theological Seminary, then known as East Windsor Hill.

In the winter of his senior year in 1841, he returned home to serve as principal at Sanderson Academy in Ashfield, where he went to school as a youth. Halfway through the completion of his study, he was licensed to preach by the Franklin County Association in Colrain, Massachusetts. He continued with his studies and would graduate in August of 1841. Six months prior to his graduation, however, he received a call to a church in Eastford, Connecticut. He accepted the call on the condition that he would first complete his seminary courses, but would occupy the pulpit on Sundays or else have it filled by someone else, even his classmates, as he wished.

It was during this time that he began preaching and met Nathaniel Lyon. Lyon, a native of Eastford, had just graduated from West Point and had returned home when he made the acquaintance of the new young pastor. Williams and Lyon became fast friends and would maintain their friendship throughout their lives. Nathaniel Lyon would climb through the ranks of the U.S. Army, rising to the rank of General. On August 10, 1861, Lyon would lead his troops into the Battle of Wilson's Creek in Missouri, where fate would make him the first Union General killed in the Civil War. His remains would eventually be returned to Eastford for burial, and his funeral conducted by his good friend, Reverend Francis Williams.

Williams was ordained at Eastford, Connecticut on September 20, 1841. Two days later, on September 22, he would marry his sweetheart, Mahala R. Badger, daughter of Enoch Badger of Springfield, Massachusetts. Together, Francis and Mahala would have five children during their ten years of ministry in Eastford. Edward arrived in 1845, followed by Charles in 1848, and their fifth child and only daughter in 1851. Two other sons before Edward had died in infancy. Shortly after daughter Mary Elizabeth's birth in 1851, the Williams family moved to Bloomfield, Connecticut, where Francis accepted a call and preached for seven years. At this time, he would also return his service to the Hartford Seminary and began serving on the Board of Trustees, a position he would hold for more than forty years, never missing a meeting. Over the next fifty years, he would miss only two of his annual seminary reunions, both absences due to his being called to preach at funerals.

At the turn of the New Year in 1858, Francis would follow his calling and move again to become the sixth pastor of the Congregational Church in Chaplin, Connecticut. On February 24, 1858, his wife's uncle, Dr. Milton Badger of New York, preached the sermon at Francis' installation. Dr. Badger was also a longtime and distinguished secretary of the Connecticut Home Missionary Society and would recruit Francis for its service, where he would serve as a director for twenty years.

In Chaplin, Francis would find permanence and serve this church and community for the next thirty-three years. During his stay in Chaplin, one hundred and fifty-seven people were received into the church either on profession of their faith or by transfer of membership. This was a remarkable credit to the pastor in those times.

In 1864, his son Edward, now nineteen, followed in his father's footsteps and enrolled at Williams College. Edward did not follow his father to the Fraternity however, which was by now called Delta Upsilon. The Williams College undergraduate chapter had voted to secede from the Anti-Secret Confederation upon a formal vote on October 6, 1863, just a year before Edward Williams enrolled. The chapter essentially began to feel that "the cause of anti-secrecy could best be served on its own campus without membership in a national society." The decision would deprive Francis Williams of a legacy, and it would be another twenty years before Delta Upsilon would officially return to campus.

Young Edward graduated from Williams with the class of 1868 and then taught for a short time, but failing health forced his return home to Chaplin, where he died on October 6, 1869 at the age of twenty-four. He was buried in the Chaplin Cemetery, just down the street from the church where his father was pastor.

In 1871, Mary Elizabeth, the Williams only daughter, followed in her father's professional footsteps as well and graduated from Mt. Holyoke Seminary. She taught school after graduation and married Reverend William H. Phipps on October 10, 1872. This happy moment was followed two years later, however, by another sad one, when Francis and Mahala's only remaining son, Charles, passed away suddenly. Charles had graduated from Eastman's Business College at Poughkeepsie, New

York. While on an engineering assignment surveying the Hudson River railroad, he had become ill and went back to Chaplin to recuperate. The illness had progressed, which resulted in a severe hemorrhage of the throat. He died at home in Chaplin on December 19, 1874, at the age of twenty-six.

The following year, the good Reverend was elected to serve in the Connecticut State House of Representatives, where he served for one term as a member of the committee on temperance, until 1876.

Williams continued to preach and serve the community of Chaplin, and enjoyed good health for his entire tenure. On April 19, 1892, two days after preaching his last sermon at the church, the Reverend Francis Williams retired from the pulpit. By the time he had finished his ministry, he had never once been out of the pulpit or missed a service on a Sunday since his ordination. After more than thirty-three years in Chaplin, Francis and Mahala moved to East Hartford to enjoy retirement.

He continued to maintain an interest in church work after his move to East Hartford and became a member at the church there. On January 2, 1896, he celebrated his eighty-second birthday and continued to be active and enjoy good health. Six days later, on Thursday, January 8, he woke as usual and attended a meeting at the church. Sometime afterward he returned home and lay down to take a nap. While napping, the good Reverend's contented heart simply quit beating. He quietly passed away of heart disease and was survived by his wife and daughter.

The following obituary from East Hartford offers a
glimpse into Francis Williams' character:

*"Of a kindly, genial disposition, every one who met Dr.
Williams could not help but like him and his sincerity
and faithfulness is shown by the long time he labored in
Chaplin where his death is deeply mourned by the entire
town. Since coming to East Hartford he has taken a
deep interest in all church work and his death will be a
loss felt by all. The funeral was held at the First
Church. President C.D. Hantraft of the Theological
Seminary spoke very feelingly for the Board of Trustees
and Rev. Mr. Moore gave a sketch of his ministerial
career. The remains were taken to Chaplin and a
funeral service was held at the Congregational Church.
A large number attended from the surrounding towns to
pay a last tribute of respect to one greatly beloved and
esteemed. Rev. Eugene M. Frary conducted the
impressive service, and a touching tribute to the life and
work of the deceased, as one filled with faithfulness,
thoroughness and completeness. The burial was in the
cemetery in sight of the church where he was so long its
faithful pastor."*

Where are they now?
A Guide to the Founders' Gravesites

Visiting a cemetery provides a gateway to the past and a connection to the future. It provides a virtual narrative of the history of our nation and the lives of its residents. A stroll through a cemetery provides one with a sense of peace, witnessing nature that is very much alive in the flora and fauna that occupy the grounds.

Some cemeteries such as Woodlawn Cemetery in New York City, Mount Auburn in Cambridge, Massachusetts, and more notable ones like Arlington National Cemetery, offer a visitor an immeasurable history lesson, both in the art and architecture, and in the history of the lives of those buried there.

Often, cemeteries themselves are sometimes neglected or forgotten, and then by default, so are those who are interred there. The purpose of this book and this section is to ensure that our Founders of Delta Upsilon Fraternity are not forgotten. Their tombstones were always meant to be lasting memorials of lives once lived.

A visit to a grave of a Founder provides an individual with an opportunity to pay their respects and to offer personal thanks to the Founding Brother for the lives that he helped mould. We may wish we could have been there on that day in November 1834, but standing at the surface of a Founder's grave somehow makes us feel as if we were.

Grave Listings by State

Note: John P. Hills and Foster Lilly are not included in the following lists since information about their final interment is unknown at the time of printing.

Connecticut
Chaplin   Francis Williams
Westchester   Hiram Bell

District of Columbia
Washington   Stephen Field
                            Zalmon Richards

Georgia
Albany   Henry Morgan

Illinois
Chicago   William Bross
Elgin   Edward Brooks

Massachusetts
Cambridge   Anson Hobart
Easthampton   Josiah Lyman
Fairhaven   Francis Tappan
Great Barrington   Algernon Baldwin
Groton   Lebbeus Phillips
Medford   George Clisby
Otis   Thomas Hall
Plainfield   Solomon Clark
Sheffield   Comfort Sparks
Springfield   Edward Clarke
                            Charles Peabody
Winchendon   Willard Brigham

New Jersey

Hillside	Lyndon Lyman
Rahway	Theophilus Page

New York

Cortlandt Manor	Daniel Brown
Huevelton	Ephraim Kellogg
Riverhead (Long Island)	Lewis Lockwood

Ohio

Cincinnati	David Pise

Washington

Seattle	Edmund Wright

Wisconsin

Kenosha	William Noble
Oakfield	Samuel Darling

Directions to the Gravesites

Any information below regarding the whereabouts of a Founder's final disposition is considered to be to the best of the author's knowledge at the time of printing. The purpose of this cemetery guide is to ensure that the location of their graves will never again be lost. The guide is designed to aid the visitor in the quick and easy location of a Founder's final resting place.

Making a pilgrimage to the grave of a Delta Upsilon Founder will provide a deeper sense of connection to the Fraternity and its founding members.

Make a personal pilgrimage. Visit as a group for a chapter retreat or service event to carefully clean and preserve a headstone. Perhaps an associate member class might take a field trip to have a stronger connection to the Founding history.

Regardless of the reason, may we never forget our Founders...

Grave of Algernon Sidney Baldwin

Algernon Sidney Baldwin

Water Street Cemetery
Corner of Route 7 and East Street
Great Barrington, Massachusetts

Brother Baldwin's resting place is among the first row of graves in the very front left section of the Water Street Cemetery in Great Barrington, Massachusetts. It is severely weathered, but still somewhat readable: "Algernon S. Baldwin, Graduate of Williams College 1836, Died Sept. 30, 1839 in the 29th year of his age."

The cemetery entrance is at the corner of Route 7 and East St. in Great Barrington. Drive just into the cemetery entrance on the corner and park. Stand at the corner of the cemetery on the left side of the entrance. Including the cement corner fence post, walk along the fence to the sixteenth post, which will be right at the pedestrian opening to the cemetery. Turn right about seven yards and you will find Baldwin's grave on the first row, three stones in, near the two trees.

Grave of Hiram Bell

Hiram Bell

Westchester Cemetery
End of Cemetery Road
Westchester, Connecticut

Brother Bell's resting place is marked by a granite
obelisk in the back corner of the Westchester Cemetery
in Westchester, Connecticut. (Township of Colchester,
Connecticut)

Using the driveway at "18 Cemetery Road" as a point of
origin, drive past the cemetery on your left to the
cemetery entrance at the end of Cemetery Rd. Once in
the cemetery entrance, drive around two left curves to
the "top of the hill" (which will be at the back of the
cemetery) and park on the left at the second main row of
graves. Find the "Peck" monument on the left side.
With the "Peck" monument on your left, walk into the
cemetery all the way to the end. Brother Bell's
monument is the last obelisk on the right, near the
cemetery edge.

Grave of Willard Brigham

Willard Brigham

Riverside Cemetery
Winchendon, Massachusetts

Brother Brigham's grave is located in the back center of
Riverside Cemetery in Winchendon, Massachusetts.
Into Winchendon, follow Route 2002/Route 12 North to
Glenallen Street and turn left over the bridge. The
cemetery entrance will be on the right about a quarter
mile down the road.

Enter the cemetery gate off of Glenallen Street. Once
inside the gate, take the straightest road option (third
fork from the left) into the center of the cemetery
(Spruce Avenue). Travel about a tenth of a mile down
Spruce Avenue, stopping at a large tree about thirty feet
before the first left turn (Pine Avenue). From the road,
looking towards the left hand side of the road, locate the
"Abbott" and "Bateman" monuments. With "Abbott" on
the left, walk approximately sixty feet into the cemetery
and you will see the Brigham plot and monument on the
left, accentuated by the headstones of the individual
graves. (Official Cemetery record: Section 521)

Marker at the Former Channing Cemetery

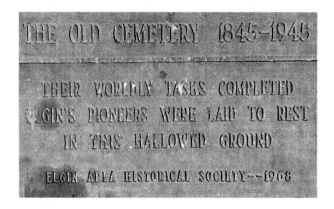

THE OLD CEMETERY 1845-1945

THEIR WORLDLY TASKS COMPLETED
ELGIN'S PIONEERS WERE LAID TO REST
IN THIS HALLOWED GROUND

ELGIN AREA HISTORICAL SOCIETY--1968

Edward Flint Brooks

Channing Cemetery (no longer exists)
63 South Channing St.
Elgin, Illinois

Sadly, with the best records available, it appears that
the whereabouts of the remains of Brother Brooks has
been lost through time. When Brother Brooks died, he
was buried in Channing Cemetery in Elgin, Illinois.
When the cemetery ran out of room, Elgin, Illinois
opened Bluff City Cemetery in 1889. Burials at
Channing Cemetery ceased right after the turn of the
century and the cemetery began to fall into a state of
disrepair. In the 1940s, officials decided to exhume the
remains of those buried in Channing Cemetery and
move them to Bluff City Cemetery. Those remains that
were not claimed were either moved, or in some cases,
"whatever remained of the remains" were simply
bulldozed as Elgin made way to use the land for the
building of an elementary school, which still exists on
the grounds today. It appears that Brother Brooks'
remains were not claimed and apparently were also not
buried elsewhere. His grave was likely bulldozed into a
mass grave, to a spot that is now forever hidden in the
lush landscape behind the school building. The
memory of Brother Brooks resides in beautiful parkland
behind Channing Memorial Elementary School, and in a
solitary rock on the school grounds that contains a
plaque, dedicated to the memory of those who were once
buried at Channing Cemetery.

Grave of William Bross

William Bross

Rosehill Cemetery
5800 Ravenswood Avenue
Chicago, Illinois

Brother Bross's resting place is in front of an impressive monument in Rosehill Cemetery in Chicago, Illinois; a cemetery in which one would find many other notable people, including former Delta Upsilon Fraternity President and United States Vice-President, Charles G. Dawes, *Marietta 1884.*

Enter the cemetery gate off of Ravenswood Ave. Once inside the gate, take an immediate left (along the front edge of the property and before you get to the roundabout). Stay on that road for approximately a tenth of a mile, keeping to the left side at the first fork in the road, taking the road nearest the pond. At the next three-way fork, take a sharp right at Section B (marker is at the corner and the "McVicar" marker will be visible as well.) The Bross monument is visible and prominent about thirty yards further down on the left side of the road.

Grave of Daniel Brown

Daniel Brown

Hillside Cemetery
1033 Oregon Road
Cortlandt Manor, New York

Brother Brown's resting place, and that of his wife and
son, is marked by a marble headstone in the front
section of Hillside Cemetery in Cortlandt Manor
(formerly just Cortlandt), New York.

Once inside the main entrance to the cemetery off of
Oregon Rd., (by the office on the left side of the entrance
road) take the first and almost immediate right turn
into the cemetery and drive along the ridge of the hill.
Drive straight, past the sharp left turn and take the
road as it curves to the left, past the "Barrett"
mausoleum. At the "end" of the road, follow it further to
the left and up the slight hill. Once at the "intersection"
of the next road on the left (marked by the "Horton"
monument), drive about sixty more feet (to the
beginning of the trees) to the "Polhill" monument on the
left side of the road. The Brown marker (upright) is
approximately seventy-five feet (six or seven rows) into
the cemetery, directly behind the "Polhill" monument.
(Official Cemetery record: #9, Block 2, Ave. B) (Knight
Plot)

Grave of Solomon Clark

Solomon Clark

Hilltop Cemetery
Intersection of North Central St. and Union
St. Plainfield, Massachusetts

Brother Clark's resting place is marked by a granite stone in the left center of the Hilltop Cemetery, located at the intersection of North Central and Union Street in Plainfield, Massachusetts.

To the left of the main auto entrance, find the steps to the central pedestrian entrance to the cemetery. The Shaw obelisk is noticeable on immediate front left. From the front edge of the top step measure approximately fifty yards straight ahead down the trail into the cemetery. Brother Clark's black granite headstone is easily visible among all of the other marble headstones on the immediate right from the trail. (Official Cemetery record: Row 22, Section 8)

Grave of Edward Clarke

Edward Clarke

Oak Grove Cemetery
426 Bay Street
Springfield, Massachusetts

Brother Clarke's resting place is marked by a short dark gray granite stone in the front right section of the Oak Grove Cemetery in Springfield, Massachusetts.

Once in the main gate off of Bay Street, drive up the center road to the intersection of the cemetery's Main Avenue. Make a hard right onto Main Avenue, past Lane Avenue and Oak Avenue Park on the right side before the road curves to the left, near a tree on the right between the "Porter" and "Shores" monuments. Clarke's grave is five rows directly behind the Porter monument. The inscription is on the side facing the main gate. (Official Cemetery record: Section 12, Lot 592)

Grave of George Clisby

George Clisby

Salem Street Burial Ground
Salem Street and Riverside Avenue
Medford, Massachusetts

Brother Clisby's grave is marked by a tablet monument
that is now weathered beyond recognition. The grave is
outlined by a shallow layer of brick, upon which the
tablet was set in 1836, by the faculty and students of
Williams College.

From the cemetery entrance off of Salem Street, walk
directly ahead (even diverting from the winding path)
approximately fifty yards to the large marble tablet
monument (third tablet behind the large obelisk near
the center of the cemetery), flat and parallel to the
ground.

Grave of Samuel Dana Darling

Samuel Dana Darling

Avoca Cemetery
Highway D
Oakfield, Wisconsin

Brother Darling and his wife Lydia are buried in a plot
intermixed with older and more recent burials. Their resting
place is marked by a single marble headstone, which contains
information for both of them. Brother Darling's headstone
indicates "S.D. Darling."

From Fond du Lac, Wisconsin, travel south on Highway 41 to
the Highway 151 bypass and turn south. Travel about two
miles to County Highway D. Turning to the left onto
Highway D, travel another three miles. About one mile past
Highway B, Highway D will curve to the right into Oakfield,
and at that curve, Avoca Cemetery will be visible on the right.
Take the first of four driveways, turning right into Avoca
Cemetery. The section immediately to the left is Section B.
(Hwy B can also be accessed by turning west off of Highway
41. About halfway to Highway D, Highway B will do a slight
jog north before going west again. Turn left at Highway D
and travel one mile to Oakfield).

Ignoring the first "maintenance road" at the edge of the
cemetery, go into the first driveway (between the first two
sections) to the very right of the cemetery. Section B will be
on the left side of this driveway. Drive in approximately
thirty yards, just past the first tree on the left. The
"Kammholz" plot will be at the roadside, immediately to the
right of the tree. Walk into the section approximately fifteen
yards. The Darling headstone is the white marble headstone,
facing the opposite direction, directly behind the "Kammholz"
plot. (Official Cemetery record: Section B, Part 3, Row 2)

Grave of Stephen Johnson Field

Stephen Johnson Field

Rock Creek Cemetery
Rock Creek Church Road
Washington, D.C.

Brother Field's grave is very easy to find and is marked
by a stout granite obelisk near the center of Rock Creek
Cemetery in Washington, D.C., where many other
notables are buried including four other Justices of the
United States Supreme Court.

Drive into the main gate off of Rock Creek Church Road.
Stay straight on the centermost road, heading towards
the church directly ahead. At the fork in the road, take
the right fork and continue along the right side of the
section that is occupied by the church itself (Section A).
On the left hand side of the road at the corner of this
section (right at the left turn which takes you onto a
road that goes behind the church) you will see the Field
plot marked by a prominent granite obelisk. (In the
back right corner of Section A, as if looking at the front
of the church). (Official Cemetery record: Section A,
Grave 184-4.)

Thomas Amory Hall's grave

Thomas Amory Hall

Otis Cemetery
Junction of Highway 8 & Highway 23
Otis, Massachusetts

Brother Hall's resting place, and that of his wife, is on
the side of a hill in Otis, Massachusetts, across the
street from the Congregational Church in Otis where he
had served as pastor. The cemetery is at the junction of
Hwy 8 and Hwy 23, just to the right of the Episcopal
Church.

Just inside the entrance, find the first large tree and/or
erosion wall on the right side of the road. From the base
of the tree, walk approximately sixty feet into the
cemetery to the tenth stone, which will be the resting
place of Hall and his wife, right behind the Norton
monument approximately six rows up the hill.

Anson Loomis Hobart's unmarked grave

Anson Loomis Hobart

Mount Auburn Cemetery
580 Mount Auburn Street
Cambridge, Massachusetts

Brother Hobart's resting place is in the historic Mount
Auburn Cemetery in Cambridge, Massachusetts, along with a
number of noted authors and poets. Former Harvard
President and fellow DU brother, James B. Conant is buried
alongside the road at 221 Willow Avenue East. Brother
Hobart himself is buried in the same section and just a stone's
throw from American poet Oliver Wendell Holmes Sr. None
of the graves in Lot 2385 are marked but the plot itself is
marked by a simple marble obelisk containing the name
"Perkins", which is his wife's family name. Brother Hobart's
wife was buried here in her family plot in 1878, so he
naturally followed her here upon his death in 1890.

The cemetery office is very helpful and maps of the cemetery
are available. Brother Hobart's grave is relatively easy to
find. Once inside the main gate off of Mount Auburn Street,
stay to the right of the cemetery office and chapel on Central
Avenue. Take an immediate left behind the chapel onto
Fountain Avenue. Drive up Fountain Avenue to the first
major left hand turn, which will be Lime Avenue. At the
immediate fork on Lime Avenue, stay to the left and park just
beyond the wrought iron fenced plot on the right. Just beyond
the fence is a plot containing many members of the Hobart
family. Just beyond this plot, along side the road, you will
find a single obelisk containing the name "Perkins". Looking
directly at the obelisk from the street, Brother Hobart's grave
would be just behind the monument and over to the right
about three grave spaces at the edge of the lot. (Official
Cemetery record: Lot 2385, Grave 5)

Ephraim William Kellogg's grave

Ephraim William Kellogg

Hillcrest Cemetery
Rensselaer Street
Heuvelton, New York

To get to the cemetery from Ogdensburg, New York,
take Hwy 812 towards Heuvelton off of Hwy 37. Once
into Heuvelton, the main entrance to Hillcrest Cemetery
is located on Rennsselaer Street in Heuvelton, in the
Town of Oswegatchie. As you enter the main entrance,
proceed approximately one-hundred-fifty feet to where
the road forks. Bear to the right and at that spot, look
to your right and the tombstone is right there near the
road.

Grave of Lewis C. Lockwood

Lewis Conger Lockwood

Riverhead Cemetery
Roanoke Avenue
Riverhead, New York

The main entrance to Riverhead Cemetery is off of
Roanoke Avenue. However, Brother Lockwood's resting
place is more easily found from the old entrance to
Riverhead Cemetery, off of Pulaski Street, near the
intersection of Pulaski Street and Griffing Avenue.
Enter the Pulaski Street entrance through the two brick
columns. From the entrance, stay straight on the main
road, avoiding any of the forks to the left. At
approximately one-hundred-fifty yards from the
entrance there will be a small avenue or drivable
"break" in the section on the left. Stop and park about
ten yards before this break and Brother Lockwood's
marble monument will be visible on the right side of the
road. Brother Lockwood and his wife and daughter are
buried in this Terry family plot, along with relatives of
his wife's family. (Official Cemetery record: Map 332,
Plot 21 in the older section of the cemetery.)

Grave of Josiah Lyman

Josiah Lyman

Main Street Cemetery
300 block of Main Street
Easthampton, Massachusetts

Brother Lyman's resting place is marked by an impressive granite cross monument in the center of the leftmost section of the Main Street Cemetery in Easthampton, Massachusetts.

Facing the cemetery from the road, enter the first driveway on the left. Stay straight through the row of trees and park halfway down the road on the left. Just past the "Pomeroy" monument you will find the Lyman family plot along the road. The large granite cross monument behind the rows of graves of the Lyman family marks the resting place of Brother Lyman and his wife. The main inscription is on reverse side of the monument, facing away from the road. (Official Cemetery record: Lot 39, Section 3.)

Grave of Lyndon Graves Lyman

Lyndon Graves Lyman

Evergreen Cemetery
1137 North Broad Street
Hillside, New Jersey

Evergreen Cemetery was considered one of the more prominent and affluent cemeteries in the late nineteenth and early twentieth centuries. It is where many of New Jersey's affluent and prominent citizens are buried. Also buried in Evergreen, in the same section but on the opposite end from Lyman, is notable DU and author Brother Stephen Crane, *Lafayette & Syracuse 1894*.

To find Brother Lyman's grave, drive into the main gate off of North Broad Street and keep right, heading toward the office building on the right. At the point where the office starts and immediately before the triangular median that highlights a flagpole, turn left into the cemetery grounds. Section D will be on the left. Drive approximately .10 mile into the cemetery. Ignoring the first possible left hand turn, go around the old brick vault, turning left at the second turn and park just after making that left. The second plot of graves after the old brick vault is the Lyman-Robb plot, which for reference, is directly across the road from the "Elliott" marker. Brother Lyman is in the third row of graves between his second wife Jane Robb and his father-in-law John Robb. Jane Robb is buried between Lyndon and her second husband Thomas McKee. (Lyman's grave marker mistakenly lists his date of death as September 10, 1871. The marker may possibly reflect the date of his burial instead. (Official Cemetery record: Section C, Lot 28.)

View of Oakview Cemetery

Henry Morgan

Oakview Cemetery
200 Cotton Avenue
Albany, Georgia

Brother Morgan's final resting place is almost certainly <u>somewhere</u> in Oakview Cemetery. Since it appears that he did not have immediate family, he was likely buried in an unmarked grave to begin with. To make matters worse in finding him, however, many of the cemetery records, and a great number of headstones were lost or destroyed in the great flood that besieged Albany in 1994. Ever since then, the cemetery management has been trying to recover as much information as possible about those buried in Oakview. Some, like Brother Morgan, have sadly been lost to time.

Grave of William Henry Noble

William Henry Noble

Green Ridge Cemetery
6604 W. 7th Avenue
Kenosha, Wisconsin

Brother Noble's resting place is marked by a modest granite ground marker in the center of the Green Ridge Cemetery in Kenosha, Wisconsin. The marker reads simply "W. Noble, C.E." The "C.E." on the marker stands for "Civil Engineer".

From the front gate of the cemetery off of 7th Avenue, drive in approximately .18 mi. About twenty-five yards before the road curves to the left at the end, notice the "Barber" marker on the right side of the road. Using the Barber marker as a point of origin on your left, walk into the cemetery to the second lot on the right where you will notice the decorative marble "Jackson" monument. Noble's plot is the fourth marker on the right approximately twenty-seven feet off the road just past the marble Jackson monument. (Official Cemetery record: Lot 2, Block 69.)

Grave of Theophilus Page

Theophilus Page

Rahway Cemetery
1670 Saint Georges Avenue
Rahway, New Jersey

Theophilus Page is buried in the historic Rahway
Cemetery, where many Revolutionary War veterans are
buried, including Abraham Clark, a signer of the
Declaration of Independence.

Cemetery records prior to the late 1960s for Rahway
Cemetery were lost in a fire several years ago and no
longer exist, but Brother Page's lone plot and marker
have been located in what is listed according to the
official cemetery record as section seven in the back part
of the cemetery grounds.

To find Brother Page's plot, enter the cemetery through
the gate off of High Street (on the Westfield Ave./Grand
Ave.) side of the cemetery, near the maintenance
garage. Once inside the gate, take the second possible
left turn at the "Ross" marker. Go down (driving or
walking) to the end of the road just as it begins to curve
to the left. Entering the grounds on the right at the
curve, just behind the "Toms" marker, walk about six
graves in to find Brother Page's simple but stately gray
granite marker, sitting alone in the small plot.

Grave of Charles Peabody

Charles Peabody

Springfield Cemetery
171 Maple Street
Springfield, Massachusetts

Brother Peabody's resting place is located in the older
section of the cemetery. If needed, an office is available
for assistance near the main entrance off of Maple
Street. However, the grave is best reached from the
Pine Street gate. If entering from the Maple Street
entrance, get directions from the office to the Pine
Street gate and use said gate as a beginning point of
reference.

From the Pine Street gate, travel straight at the
immediate intersection. Drive approximately thirty
yards to the center of the section and park on the right.
Find the "Russell" monument and walk into the
cemetery about twenty yards, approximately nine rows
in, to the Peabody grave, which will be found right in
front of the brown "Collins" obelisk. (Official Cemetery
record: Lot 15.)

Lebbeus Rude Phillips

Cremated
Groton, Massachusetts

At the time of his death, Brother Phillips was living in
Roxbury, Massachusetts, but died while visiting friends
in Amherst. All indications point to Groton,
Massachusetts as his place of burial, however there is
no record of his final place of interment. The best
research indicates that he was likely cremated as were
his wife and many members of his family. It is likely
that his ashes were scattered in Groton, Massachusetts,
where he may have had a summer home.

David Pise

Spring Grove Cemetery
4521 Spring Grove Avenue
Cincinnati, Ohio

Brother Pise's resting place is marked by a unique stone monument in the form of a "log cross" sitting on a pedestal in section 110, the center of the Spring Grove Cemetery in Cincinnati, Ohio.

The gate to Spring Grove is the one with an historic office immediately to the right of the gate. Directions start from this gate, <u>not</u> from the gate to the Jon Deitloff Funeral Center, which is adjacent to the west edge of the cemetery. Drive into the gate of Spring Grove and follow the white dotted line straight ahead approximately .7 miles under the bridge and up the hill. At about the .7 mile point, you will notice a stone shelter on the right. Just past this shelter, begin to look for the unique "log cross" monument on the left side of the road between the Koehler monument and the water spigot. The "log cross" monument marks the resting place of Brother Pise and some of his family. Brother Pise's grave is immediately behind and right center of the monument, covered by a blanket of English ivy in the shade of an American Hornbeam tree. (Official Cemetery record: Section 110, Lot 263, Space 5)

Grave of David Pise

Zalmon Richards

Oak Hill Cemetery
3001 R Street NW
Washington, D.C.

Brother Richards is buried in the old and quaint Oak Hill Cemetery in Washington, D.C., where many of Washington's more notable and historical citizens are buried. A trip to Oak Hill should be planned in advance, however, as the cemetery grounds are only open to the public for about six hours a day, Monday through Friday, and a short time on Sundays. Oak Hill is closed on Saturdays, holidays and when there is a funeral in progress. The roads inside the cemetery are one-lane and the terrain is very sloping. Fortunately, Brother Richards' grave is <u>very</u> easy to find. The directions below are based on reaching the grave by <u>walking</u>, once inside the gate.

Once inside the main gate by the office, take the immediate right down the path inside the gate, essentially walking along the fence line the entire way. As the road begins to curve left by the chapel, continue straight and walk down the set of steps, still along the fence line. Continue walking straight down the narrow path (ledge) until you reach the path "intersection" where the fence line "turns" to the right (essentially at the other vehicle gate of the cemetery.) Look to the right side of the path at the "corner" of the fence line and you will see Brother Richards grave marker immediately. If you reach the "Russell" monument on the left of the path, you have gone too far. (Official Cemetery record: Lot 669, Site 10.) *Note: The large obelisk directly across the path, about ten feet from Richard's grave, is the grave of Edwin M. Stanton, President Abraham Lincoln's noted Secretary of War who said, "Now he belongs to the ages", upon the death of Lincoln.*

Grave of Zalmon Richards

Comfort Sparks

Bow Wow Cemetery
Bow Wow Road
Sheffield, Massachusetts

Brother Sparks' resting place is marked by a simple
marble headstone at the back of the Bow Wow
Cemetery, located at Bow Wow Road in Sheffield,
Massachusetts. Brother Sparks' headstone has been
broken once already, and at the time of this book
printing, had been re-entered into the soil and was
leaning immediately in front of its original base.
Weather has taken its toll on this marble headstone,
which is barely readable. Brother Sparks is buried to
the immediate left of his mother, and his father
"Deacon" Comfort Sparks.

Turn onto Miller Road off of Route 7 in Sheffield. Go 3.5
miles down the road (becomes Bow Wow Road), staying
left at the first fork, and then right at the second fork
around the pond. Keep straight at the third fork after
the paved road ends and becomes a gravel/dirt road.
Travel approximately .4 miles to the cemetery on the
right, staying to the left at the final fork. From the
main gate of the cemetery, walk straight in about sixty
yards towards the back of the cemetery, just past the
row of four pine trees. The grave of Comfort Sparks is
the third stone from the end on the right.

Grave of Comfort Sparks

Francis Wilder Tappan

Riverside Cemetery
274 Main Street
Fairhaven, Massachusetts

Brother Tappan's resting place is marked by a
headstone at the front of the Riverside Cemetery,
located in Fairhaven, Massachusetts. Brother Tappan's
headstone is very easy to find, not far from the main
entrance.

Just inside the main gate, the cemetery office/house is
visible on the right. Go down the road a little bit, and at
the first fork in the road, notice a "Rules and
Regulations" sign posted on the right side of the road.
Brother Tappan's headstone is easily found behind that
sign, just off of the edge of the road. (Official Cemetery
record: Lot 12, Section 4)

Grave of Francis Wilder Tappan

Francis Williams

Chaplin Cemetery
Near the Library at 130 Chaplin Street
Chaplin, Connecticut

Brother Williams's resting place is in the back left
section of the old Chaplin Cemetery in Chaplin,
Connecticut, just down the street from the
Congregational Church where he had served as pastor.

Turn left onto Chaplin St. from CT Route 198. Park in
the library lot on the left by the cemetery. Go into the
walk-in "break" in the stone wall at the corner of the
cemetery nearest the library and Chaplin St. Walk
straight ahead to almost the back edge of the cemetery.
Williams' monument is the last granite obelisk on the
left, and is on the second level down, just past the
"Clark" Monument.

Grave of Francis Williams

Edmund Wright

Lake View Cemetery
1554 15th Avenue E
Seattle, Washington

The resting places of Brother Wright and his wife
Achsah are marked with matching gray granite
headstones, separated by a large square-shaped shrub
in the west end of the cemetery, about four-tenths of a
mile into the cemetery grounds.

Enter the cemetery through the main gate on the east
side of the cemetery, off of 15th Ave. E. Once inside the
gate, take the first left into the cemetery grounds, which
heads south for a short bit before resuming west and
curving to the right (north). Take the next left turn
opportunity, which will head due west further up into
the cemetery. At about three-tenths of a mile into the
entire trip from the main gate, the road will begin to
curve to the right. After the slight curve to the right,
stay straight ahead, just past the first right turn
opportunity and park along the road side about four
plots into the section. Walk about twenty yards into the
section on the right side of the road. Brother Wright's
plot is very visible in the south-center portion of this
section. (Official Cemetery record: Lot 250)

Grave of Edmund Wright

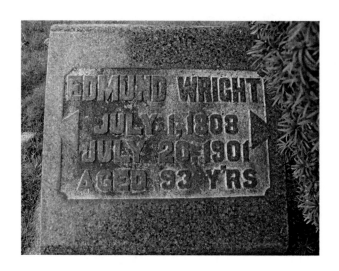

293

Review Questions
Part One

1. Name the titles of the Fraternity's 50th, 100th, and 150th year history books.

2. What is the name of the Fraternity's official magazine?

3. In what year did a fire destroy the early records of the Fraternity? In what building did the fire occur?

4. What was the name of the member manual prior to The Cornerstone?

5. How many of the Fraternity's thirty Founders sought a career in ministry?

6. Who was President of the United States in 1834?

7. How many U.S. States existed in 1834?

8. Approximately how much was a semester's tuition at Williams College in 1834?

9. Give four reasons why an 1834 college student might choose Williams College for an education.

10. Name the room where the Fraternity's Founding took place in 1834. On what floor was this room?

11. Name the building at Williams College that housed the room referred to in question 10 that primarily housed the freshman and sophomore students.

12. Name the two secret societies that existed on the Williams College campus in 1834 prior to the non-secret Founding.

13. Which of the two secret societies provided the impetus for the non-secret formation?

14. Name the two societies that made up the Adelphic Union.

15. What did the students who opposed the secret fraternities wear that mocked the secret fraternities?

16. Name at least one circumstance that provided the impetus to enact change and begin the non-secret Fraternity?

17. What were the main desires the men hoped to achieve by starting the Fraternity?

18. Where was the idea of a non-secret fraternity first discussed? (name room, resident and building)

19. Name the three sophomores who first formally discussed the formation of a non-secret fraternity.

20. Name the Fraternity's founding date.

21. On what day of the week was this date?

22. What was the name chosen by the Founders as the first name for the organization which later became Delta Upsilon.

23. What percentage of the Williams College student body joined the effort on the day of the Founding?

24. Who was elected the first president of the new non-secret society?

25. What percentage of the Williams College student body were members of the non-secret fraternity within two years?

Review Questions
Part Two

1. Which three Founders were essentially the first organizers of the non-secret effort that led to the formation of DU?

2. Who recruited the first new member following the November 4th Founding?

3. Who was the first Founder to have a legacy follow him into the Fraternity?

4. Which Founder also founded a second national organization? What organization was it?

5. Which two Founders are credited as the authors of the Fraternity's first Constitution?

6. What two Founders celebrated a birthday on November 4th, the day the Fraternity was founded?

7. Which Founder later served on the U.S. Supreme Court, serving over 34 years on that bench?

8. Which Founder was a confirmed abolitionist, and was essentially responsible for the eventual establishment of Hampton University in Virginia?

9. Which Founder was chief editor of the *Chicago Tribune* newspaper for several years?

10. Which Founder died alone on his birthday?

11. Which three Founders became judges?

12. Which Founder served as a state lieutenant governor?

13. Who was the only Founder to have his own son follow him as a member of the Fraternity?

14. Which Founder essentially helped to rebuild Chicago after the "Great Chicago Fire" of 1871?

15. Who was the only Founder known to have traveled to Canada?

16. What Founder taught a future U.S. President? Which U.S. President was it?

17. Which Founder's younger brother actually became a Founding Father of a different DU Chapter? Which Chapter?

18. Which Founder was one of the first people in America to engage in the then relatively new profession of dentistry?

19. Which Founder is the only one known to have received a United States patent?

20. Besides the Founder in question 18, who was the only other Founder to engage in the practice of medicine?

21. Which Founder was a close friend of Abraham Lincoln?

22. Who was the only Founder actually born in Williamstown, Massachusetts?

23. Who were the youngest and oldest Founders on November 4, 1834. What were their ages?

24. What was the penalty, should a member of the non-secret fraternity decide to later join one of the secret societies?

25. What was the main purpose of the societies <u>meetings</u> after the Founding?

Appendix

For more information on this book, or to purchase additional copies, contact the Fraternity, or visit the book's website at:

https://www.createspace.com/3360786

For more information about the Delta Upsilon Fraternity, visit: www.DeltaU.org

For more information about the Delta Upsilon Foundation, visit: www.DUEF.org

Mailing Address for the Fraternity and Foundation:

8705 Founders Road
Indianapolis, IN 46268

To download a free e-book copy of Lewis C. Lockwood's book: *Mary S. Peake: The Colored Teacher at Fortress Monroe* visit:

http://www.gutenberg.org/etext/20744

Please send updates or corrections to:
Mr. Craig Sowell
c/o Delta Upsilon Fraternity
8705 Founders Road
Indianapolis, IN 46268

32	30	28	26
Clark Clarke			
31	29	27	25

FOURTH FLOOR SOUTH

18	20	22	24
Morgan			Field
17	19	21	23

FOURTH FLOOR NORTH

10	12	14	16
	Noble Sparks	Page	
	Brown L. Lyman	Lockwood	
9	11	13	15

THIRD FLOOR NORTH

2	4	6	8
Hills	Bross		
Brooks Peabody	Lilly Williams	Brigham	
1	3	5	7

SECOND FLOOR NORTH

S ⟵――――――――――――⟶ N

Author's rendition of West College dorm room assignments for freshmen and sophomores in 1834. *Note: Thomas Hall is not listed because he was not listed in the 1834 rooming list.*

300

Preamble and Constitution of the Social Fraternity

Arguably, this single piece of information provides more than anything else, the greatest insight into what exactly happened on November 4, 1834. Or at the very least, it paints a vivid picture as to what was on the minds of the thirty men that evening. The Constitution itself was completed by Founders Daniel Brown and Edward Clarke. The Preamble was largely the work of E. P. Hawkes of the Class of 1838. While not an original Founder, Hawkes joined the effort as part of the "first recruits". His Preamble and the Constitutional sections of Brown and Clark resulted in a final collaboration that was first printed in 1837, and reproduced below.

Preamble

Believing that secret societies are calculated to destroy the harmony of college, to create distinctions not founded on merit, to produce strife and animosity; we feel called upon to exert ourselves to counteract the evil tendency of such associations.

We believe that the evils resulting from them are such as can be suppressed only by action combined with principle. We are not among the number of those who would "level down" but we would "level up." We would invest no class of our fellow students with factitious advantage, but would place all upon an equal footing in running the race of honorable distinction.

The only superiority which we acknowledge is the superiority of merit.

We therefore, members of Williams College – believing that voluntary associations, if properly conducted, exert a mighty influence in the correction of evil – do agree to form ourselves into a society for the purpose of counteracting the evil tendency of secret associations, for maintaining and diffusing liberal principles, and for promoting the great objects of social and literary improvement.

In doing this, we are confident that we have at least the best interests of the institution to which we belong, and that we are directed by the light of experience, the suggestions of reason and the dictates of conscience.[42]

We adopt the following Constitution as our guide

Section 1st

Art. 1st: This Society shall be called the Social Fraternity of Williams College

Art. 2nd: The officers of this Society shall consist of a President, Vice-President, Secretary/Treasurer, Corresponding Secretary, two Critics and Reader; and these shall be chosen by ballot.[43]

Art. 3rd: The President shall preside at all regular meetings of the Society, shall have power at any emergency to call an extra meeting, shall be expected to

---

[42] This paragraph was added in 1840.
[43] By 1840, the Critics and the Reader were removed as officers.

deliver an address at the expiration of his term of office: and in his absence, the highest officer present shall fulfill his duties.[44]

Art. 4th: The Secretary/Treasurer shall keep a record of the proceedings of the Society and the Corresponding Secretary shall carry on all its correspondence. The other officers shall transact the business usually devolving upon their offices.

Section 2nd

Art. 1st: No person shall be admitted a member of this Society who belongs to, or countenances any secret society in this College.

Art. 2nd: A candidate may be admitted a member at any regular meeting by a concurrence of two-thirds of the members present.

Art. 3rd: Any member in good standing may at any constitutional meeting, and in accordance with the provisions of the fourth article of this section, receive an honorable dismission [sic].

Art. 4th: All applications for dismission shall be laid over to any subsequent meeting which the Society may appoint that shall be held within two weeks from the time of application.

---

[44] By 1840, the "highest officer" was changed to specifically name the Vice-President as the one who would fulfill duties in the absence of the President.

Art. 5th: If any member shall join or countenance any secret association of this College he shall be <u>expelled</u> from the Society.

Art. 6th: This society shall not recognize society divisions but real merit in College elections.

Section 3rd

Art. 1st: The meetings of this Society shall be uniformly held once in two weeks, on Tuesday evenings, commencing with the first Tuesday of each term at such place as the officers shall provide.[45]

Art. 2nd: The exercises of the Society shall be literary – consisting of compositions, orations and debates – and shall not at any meeting continue more than one hour, unless by vote of the Society.

Art. 3rd: Each member shall be bound to attend all meetings of the Society, and fulfill all his appointments by his honor as a gentleman.

Art. 4th: The officers of the Society shall be chosen at the last meeting of each term.

Art. 5th: This Constitution may be altered or amended at any regular meeting, by a concurrence of two-thirds of the members present.[46]

---

[45] By 1840, the meeting schedule was changed for meetings to be held once a week instead of once every two weeks.

[46] By 1840, a proposition to the constitution was required to have "lain on the table" for at least one week before it could be amended.

Art. 6th: This Constitution shall be read at the first
meeting of each term.

The First Pledge

You affirm upon your honor that the principles of this
Society as expressed in its Preamble and Constitution
accord entirely with your views and you pledge yourself
faithfully to adhere to them.

Founder Facts

Founder Legacies

Josiah Lyman
>Brother - Addison Lyman, *Williams 1839*
>Brother - Horace Lyman, *Williams 1842*

Edmund Wright
>Brother – Russell Wright, *Williams 1841*

Foster Lilly
>Brother - Aruna Hall Lilly, *Williams 1848*

Zalmon Richards
>Son – George Richards, *Williams 1904*

Francis Williams
>Brother – Fordyce Williams, *Rochester 1853*[47]

Founders who served as Chapter President

Anson Hobart	1834-1835
Ephraim Kellogg	1835-1836
David Pise	1836-1837
Francis Williams	1837-1838

Founders who were Class Valedictorian
Field

---

[47] Fordyce Williams was a Founder of the Rochester Chapter

Founders who were Class Salutatorian
Hall

Founders who were Phi Beta Kappa
Bross, Field, Hall and Pise (honorary)

First Founder to die
Clisby (1836)

Last Founder to die
Lockwood (1904)

Ages at the time of the Founding

28	Phillips	21	Brigham
			Bross
27	Darling		Hall
			Page
26	Bell		Sparks
	Wright		
		20	Brown
24	Clarke		Morgan
	Hills		Williams
	L. Lyman		
	Peabody	19	Hobart
			Pise
23	Baldwin		
	Clark	18	Clisby
	Kellogg		Field
	J. Lyman		Lockwood
	Richards		
		17	Noble
22	Brooks		
	Lilly	16	Tappan

Founder's Birthdays[48]

January 2	Francis Williams
January 8	Henry Morgan
January 29	John Hills
February 7	Samuel Darling
March 2	Algernon Baldwin
March 2	Solomon Clark
May 2	Ephraim Kellogg
May 4	Willard Brigham
May 22	William Noble
June 6	Foster Lilly
June 14	Lyndon Lyman
July 1	Charles Peabody
July 1	Edmund Wright
July 4	Theophilus Page
July 10	Edward Clarke
July 23	Daniel Brown
August 11	Zalmon Richards
August 26	George Clisby
September 2	Thomas Hall
September 27	Edward Brooks
September 29	David Pise
October 9	Josiah Lyman
November 1	Lebbeus Phillips
November 4	William Bross
November 4	Stephen Field
November 12	Anson Hobart
December 16	Hiram Bell
December 20	Lewis Lockwood
December 29	Francis Tappan

---

[48] List does not include Comfort Sparks, whose birth date is unknown.

About the Author

Craig S. Sowell is a native of Houston, Texas and is a graduate of the Conrad N. Hilton College of Hotel and Restaurant Management at the University of Houston.

After 12 years in the hospitality industry he worked in many capacities with the Delta Upsilon Fraternity and Educational Foundation in Indianapolis, Indiana. He and his wife Robin have two children.

An active DU volunteer since graduation, he has served the Fraternity is a variety of volunteer capacities, both on chapter and International Fraternity levels. He maintains a genuine love of history and an intense passion for Delta Upsilon, which resulted in his appointment as Fraternity Historian for Delta Upsilon in 2003 by Chairman Bill Messick, *Lafayette '68*.

Revealing the Non-Secrets is the result of fifteen years of thought, eight years of research and more than two years of writing. It is his first published book.

Proceeds from this book benefit both the Delta Upsilon Foundation and the Fraternity.

311

Photo Credits

By the Author

All photos in the "Where are they now?" section by the author, with the exception of:

Bibliography

Ancestry.com. 20 Oct. 2008 <http://www.ancestry.com/>.

Brown, Sylvia K. "The Adelphic Union." Archives and Special Collections. 12
    Oct. 2006. Williams College. 1 Nov. 2007
    <http://archives.williams.edu/?n=adelphic+union>.

Carpenter, Russell F. "The Brothers Field." Williams Alumni Review Mar.
    2006: 16-22.

Clarke, Julia S. High on a Hill: The Story of Christ Church Glendale. 1865-
    1965. Glendale, OH: R.H. Carruthers, 1965. 47-102.

"Death of Lyndon Lyman." Newark Daily Advertiser 6 Sept. 1871.

"Death of Zalmon Richards." The Washington Post 2 Nov. 1899: 9.

Delaney, Edmund. "Haddam's fabulous Field family." The Middletown Press
    20 July 1992: 11.

Delta Upsilon Bound Quarterlies 1882-1904. Indianapolis, IN: Delta Upsilon
    Fraternity.

Delta Upsilon Quinquennial Catalogue: 1834 - 1884. 1+.

Durfree, Calvin. Williams College Biographical Annals. Boston, Lee and
    Shepard, 1871.

Elgin Presbyterian Church History. 1917. 41-43.

Fairbanks, Wilson L., ed. Delta Upsilon Quinquennial Catalogue: 1891. New
    York, NY: Delta Upsilon Fraternity, 1891. 1+.

Geer, Curtis M. Hartford Theological Seminary - 1834-1934. Hartford, CT:
    Case, Lockwood & Brainard, 1934.

Historical Background of Dougherty County; 1836-1940. Cherokee Company, 1981.

History of Cincinnati and Hamilton County. 29 Apr. 2005
<http://www.heritagepursuit.com/hamilton/hamiltonbio971.htm>.

Lewis, R. C., ed. Williams 1793 - 1993: A Pictorial History. Williamstown, MA: Williams College Bicentennial Commission, 1993. 27.

"Luminaries." National Education Association. 20 Oct. 2008
<http://www.nea.org/aboutnea/zrichards.html>.

McNabney, George F. "Six Killed in 1867." Daily Dispatch - Moline Illinois 26 June 1937: 2.

"Noble Obituary." Kenosha Telegraph 16 May 1867.

Perry, Arthur L. Williamstown and Williams College. Perry, Arthur L., 1904.

Perry, Edward F. "Go To Chicago." Lake Forest College Alumni Bulletin: 13-14.

Rootsweb. 20 Oct. 2008 <http://www.rootsweb.ancestry.com/>.

Rudolph, Frederick. Mark Hopkins and the Log: Williams College, 1836-1872. Yale, 1956. 106-08.

Sawyer, Robinson A. "The Elimination of Fraternities at Williams College." Thesis. 23 May 2003. Williams College. 30 Sept. 2007
<http://library.williams.edu/theses/>.

"Terrible Calamity." Rocky's Archive. Feb. 2004. Hampton Historical Society.
<http://www.hamptonhistory.org/feb2004.htm>.

Williams College Obituary Records 1836-1904. Williamstown, MA: Williams College.

Williams, Paul K. "Scenes from the Past..." Aug. 2006. Mar. 2007

    <http://www.washingtonhistory.com/scenespast/images/sp_0806.pdf

    .>.

Review Answers
Part One

1. **50th** – <u>Quinquennial Catalogue</u>; **100th** – <u>Delta Upsilon: One Hundred Years</u>; **150th** – <u>Challenge, Conflict and Change: The First 150 Years of Delta Upsilon Fraternity</u>
2. *The Delta Upsilon Quarterly*
3. 1841. East College
4. <u>Our Record</u>
5. Twenty-One
6. Andrew Jackson
7. Twenty-Four
8. Twelve Dollars
9. a. Affordability; b. Convenient Location; c. Remoteness (less distraction); d. Good reputation for students desiring a career in the ministry
10. The Freshman Recitation Room on the second floor
11. West College
12. Kappa Alpha Society and Sigma Phi
13. Kappa Alpha Society
14. Philologian and Philotechnian Societies
15. Brass, inscriptionless triangle pins
16. The arrogance and oppression of the secret societies; the desire for a broader but more closely knit literary group; the desire for restoration of the atmosphere and "fabric" of the college
17. Literary improvement and intellectual stimulation of its members; fairness and equality in student affairs.
18. Francis Tappan's room, Room 22 in East College
19. Stephen Field, Lewis Lockwood and Francis Tappan
20. November 4, 1834
21. Tuesday
22. The Social Fraternity
23. A little over twenty-five percent. (30 divided by 119)
24. Anson Hobart
25. Sixty-Seven percent (Two-thirds)

Review Answers

Part Two

1. Stephen Field, Lewis Lockwood and Francis Tappan
2. Ephraim Kellogg recruited Philo Canfield as the first member to join after the Founding.
3. Josiah Lyman. His brother, Addison Lyman, *Williams 1839*
4. Zalmon Richards. National Education Association
5. Daniel Brown and Edward Clarke
6. William Bross and Stephen Field
7. Stephen Field
8. Lewis Lockwood
9. William Bross
10. Henry Morgan
11. Stephen Field, Henry Morgan and Francis Tappan
12. William Bross
13. Zalmon Richards. His son, George Richards, *Williams 1904*
14. William Bross
15. Foster Lilly
16. David Pise taught future U.S. President Grover Cleveland.
17. Francis Williams's younger brother Fordyce Williams, *Rochester 1853* founded the Rochester Chapter.
18. Lyndon Lyman
19. Josiah Lyman. In fact, he received no less than <u>six</u> patents from 1858 to 1877 for various drafting instruments.
20. Anson Hobart
21. William Bross
22. William Henry Noble
23. Oldest – Lebbeus Phillips, 28
    Youngest – Francis Tappan, 16
24. They were expelled from the Social Fraternity.
25. Literary improvement of the members. (Section 3, Article 2 of the Constitution)